A Treasury of

TURKISH FOLKTALES

For Bette Ripke,
with my warmest best wishes
Barbara K. Walker
June 16, 1992

A Treasury of

TURKISH FOLKTALES
FOR CHILDREN

Retold by Barbara K. Walker, Curator
Archive of Turkish Oral Narrative
Texas Tech University

Linnet • Books • 1988

First published as a Linnet Book,
an imprint of The Shoe String Press, Inc.,
Hamden, Connecticut 06514

A note on the texts, supplying information
about previous publication, is at the back
of this book.

The paper in this publication meets the
minimum requirements of the American
National Standard for Information Sciences
—Permanence of Paper for Printed
Library Materials, ANSI Z39.48–1984. ∞

Library of Congress Cataloging-in-Publication Data
Walker, Barbara K.
  A treasury of Turkish folktales for children.
  Summary: Thirty-four Turkish folk tales about
jinns and giants, padişahs and peasants, and beloved
heroes such as Keloğlan the bald boy.
  1. Tales—Turkey. [1. Folklore—Turkey] I. Title.
PZ8.1.W128Tr 1988   398.2'09561   88–6859
ISBN 0–208–02206–6 (alk. paper)

Printed in the United States of America

For my husband,
constant companion in the quest

Verdiğin sende kalır

———————

What you give away,
you keep

—*Turkish proverb*

Contents

Turkish riddles are sprinkled throughout the text

To the Reader   xi

Guide to Turkish Pronunciation   xv

ANIMALS IN ACTION

The Mouse and the Elephant   1
Who's There? And What Do You Want?   4
Hasan, the Heroic Mouse-Child   8
The Magpie and the Milk   11

FABLES

The Mosquito and the Water Buffalo   14
The Rabbit and the Wolf   15
The Lion's Den   16
The Crow and the Snake   17

KELOĞLAN TALES

Lazy Keloğlan and the Sultan's Daughter   20
The Three Brothers and the Hand of Fate   23
Keloğlan and the Twelve Dancing Princesses   29

Contents

NASREDDIN HOCA TALES

I Know What *I'll* Do	36
Nasreddin Hoca, Seller of Wisdom	37
Nasreddin Hoca and the Third Shot	43
The Hoca as Tamerlane's Tax Collector	45
The Hoca and the Candle	47

WITCHES, GIANTS, JINNS, AND DRAGONS

Teeny-Tiny and the Witch-Woman	49
Karaçor and the Giants	52
The Wonderful Pumpkin	62
The Courage of Kazan	67

FOOLS, FUNNY FELLOWS, TRICKSTERS, AND RIDDLERS

Just Say *Hiç*!	76
How Deli Kept His Part of the Bargain	80
Two Fools and the Gifts for Mehmet	85
Three Tricksters and the Pot of Butter	88
Trousers Mehmet and the Sultan's Daughter	91

THE HAND OF FATE

Stargazer to the Sultan	98
The Bird of Fortune	108
The Princess and the Pig	114
The Princess and the Goatherd	118
Hamal Hasan and the Baby Day	123

Contents

THEY HAD THEIR WISHES FULFILLED . . .

The Round Sultan and the Straight Answer	127
A Mirror, a Carpet, and a Lemon	132
New Patches for Old	135
Hasan and Allah's Greatness	139

Glossary 149

A Note on the Texts 154

To the Reader

Folktales are told by people who like to listen to, remember, and pass along good stories. "Folk" are not just country people; dressmakers, teachers, town mayors, librarians, janitors, and children—especially children—enjoy sharing old stories and getting new ones.

Some of the world's best folktales are still being told today, and cultures are thereby being preserved in languages most English-speaking people don't understand. To capture such tales, someone needs to learn those other languages, go and make friends of people in those other lands, and catch those special stories on tape before they are lost entirely. I am that kind of storycatcher, and the country I like best for storycatching is Turkey, a quarter of the way around the world from my home.

I am not Turkish, and neither is my husband. But we do understand and speak Turkish, and we thoroughly enjoy the Turks and their culture. For twenty-seven years, beginning in 1961, we and our Turkish colleagues have been tape recording wonderful tales in Turkish all across that country. In addition to the full school year my husband and I first spent teaching and storycatching there, we have each been back to Turkey six times, and each time we collected more good folktales on tape. Now we have more than 3,000 Turkish tales stored on tape in the Archive of Turkish Oral Narrative, housed in Texas Tech University Library in Lubbock, Texas—the largest collection of "caught-alive" Turkish tales in the world.

When you listen to these tapes, you can hear donkeys braying, dogs barking, traffic rumbling, and muezzins chanting the call to prayer, as well as the storytellers themselves, because we collected whenever and wherever storytellers were willing to talk into our microphones. You can hear sheepbells clanking and sheepdogs barking as my husband and his research partner Ahmet Uysal recorded "The Courage of Kazan" from a shepherd tending his flock in a meadow in the province of Konya in central Turkey. On the tape for "Teeny-Tiny and the Witch-Woman" you can hear the clinking of spoons against tea glasses as I caught that story from a very old woman at a party in İstanbul; as a child, she had heard the story from her grandmother in a village in the Taurus Mountains. Some of our best giant and dragon tales came from prisoners in Sinop Penitentiary, at the edge of the Black Sea, where more than a hundred "lifers" crowded around the tape recorders to share the folktales they liked best. You can hear roosters crowing beyond the walls.

Having the tales on tape is essential for retelling them because the voices of the storytellers express the real "tune" and flavor of Turkish tale-telling, with its nonsense-jingle beginnings, its many rhyming words, its spicy proverbs, the excitement or suspense or joy the teller expresses, and the rich variety in endings. Honest retelling is *not* simply a word-for-word translation into English. The "juices" that give a Turkish tale its distinctive flavor have no exact English equivalents, so a reteller must work patiently to recreate the spirit and the singing quality of the Turkish original. The work is well worthwhile, because each tale then becomes as true to oral form and as much fun for you to read or hear in English as it is for me to hear in Turkish. Also, each tale becomes a minimessenger, carrying the news that people around the world have much the same fears and hopes and dangers and dreams that you have; heroes and cowards, honest men and thieves, kindhearted folks and cruel ones, clever fellows and dummers are to be found wherever we turn. It's the flavor of the retelling that makes the Turkish version of "Twelve Dancing Princesses" different from its cousins in other countries, and that adds freshness to "The Magpie and the Milk," a Turkish variant of "The Old Woman and Her Pig," or "The Courage of Kazan," recognizable as a variant of "The Brave Little Tailor" story found in other folk collections.

The Turkish proverb "What you give away, you keep" provides the best possible reason for sharing these treasures from Turkey. Each time you give one of these tales away by sharing it, you seal it ever more firmly in your own mind and heart. In that way, you too can keep the treasures that Turkish folktales offer.

Guide to Turkish Pronunciation

Sounded as in English: *b, d, f, l, m, n, p, t, v, z*

Not used at all: *w, x*

Difficult sound to make: *ğ;* easiest way: Lengthen the sound of the vowel that comes just before it (example: *yoğurt*) and skip the *ğ*

Rest of Turkish alphabet:

a as *o* in *hobby*   Turkish example: h*a*m*a*m (Turkish bath)
c as *j* in *jam*   Turkish example: ho*c*a (Muslim teacher)
ç as *ch* in *checkers*   Turkish example: boh*ç*a (container for carrying towels, soap, and clean clothes to Turkish bath)
e as *e* in *pet*   Turkish example: D*e*h! (Giddap!)
g as *g* in *goat*   Turkish example: kar*g*a (crow)
h as *h* in *happy*   Turkish example: *h*amal (porter)
ı as *u* in *fun*   Turkish example: g*ı*dg*ı*d g*ı*dak (clucking made by hen as soon as she has laid an egg)
i as *i* in *pitch*   Turkish example: h*i*ç (nothing)
j as *s* in *treasure*   Turkish example: e*j*der (dragon)
k as *k* in *kitten*   Turkish example: *k*eloğlan (bald boy)
o as *o* in *goat*   Turkish example: h*o*roz (cock, or rooster)
ö as *ir* in *girl*   Turkish example: k*ö*se (beardless villain)
r as *r* in *run*   Turkish example: *r*ahat (comfortable, at peace)
s as *s* in *sing*   Turkish example: *s*akal (beard)

ş as *sh* in *ship*	Turkish example: padişah (king, or ruler)
u as *u* in *full*	Turkish example: yufka (thin, unleavened bread)
ü as *ew* in *few*	Turkish example: üç (three)
y as *y* in *yes*	Turkish example: yılan (snake)

NOTE: The stress on syllables in Turkish is quite even. If any syllable in a Turkish word is stressed, it is usually the *last* syllable.

The Mouse and the Elephant

Once a small proud mouse lived in a corner of the forest. While other mice scurried about, afraid of their own shadows, he sat idly twirling his whiskers. From time to time, he stamped upon the earth and then put his ear to the ground and listened. Do you know why? He wished to see whether the earth trembled!

He laughed at the notion that anyone else could be as great and powerful as he was. One day his uncle said wisely, "Watch yourself, young one. The elephant has heard about your showing off and he is very angry."

"The elephant!" scoffed the little one, who had never seen an elephant. "Who is he? I'll show him who is master of this forest!"

His uncle, old and experienced, smiled behind his paw. "There is something to be said for size. But you must see for yourself, I suppose."

"I shall teach that elephant a lesson," declared the small one. And off he set. He walked and he walked, till he came upon a lizard.

"Hey, you," called the mouse. "Are you the elephant?"

"No, no, not I," answered the lizard. "I am only a lizard."

"In that case, you may count yourself lucky," said the mouse. "If you had been the elephant, I would have broken you to bits."

The lizard, who had seen the elephant, shook with laughter. When the mouse heard the lizard laugh, he stamped his paw with rage. As it chanced, at that moment there came a great clap of thunder. The lizard, thinking the mouse had made all that noise, scuttled away under a bush. Puffing out his chest with pride, the mouse walked on.

In a little while he saw a cockroach. "Ho, there!" he called. "Are you the elephant?"

"No, no, not I," answered the cockroach. "I am only a cockroach."

"In that case, you may count yourself lucky," said the mouse. "If you had been the elephant, I would have broken you to bits."

The cockroach, who had seen the elephant, shrugged his shoulders. When the mouse saw the cockroach shrug his shoulders, he glared angrily. Just as he glared, there came a flash of lightning. The cockroach, frightened, scurried away. And the mouse, puffing out his chest even more, walked on.

A little farther on, he saw a dog. "See how slowly and sadly he walks," said the mouse to himself. "It is the elephant, and he must have heard that I was coming or he would not look so sad. Ho, there, elephant!" he called out.

"Elephant!" the dog exclaimed. "I am not the elephant. I am only a dog." And he smiled clear across his face.

"Oh, you may safely smile," said the mouse. "But if you had been the elephant, I would have broken you to bits."

Just as the dog was about to answer, a man called to him. "That is my master," said he. "For all I know, he is master of the whole world."

"Take that back!" shouted the mouse. "*I* am master of the whole world." But the dog had run off, and there was no one to hear his boast.

Still angry, the mouse went on. Suddenly he came to what looked as big as a mountain. It was gray. It stood on four legs as large as tree trunks. It had two tails, one in front and one in back. It had two great ears. Yes, it was the elephant.

"Hey, you!" called the mouse. "Are you the elephant?"

The elephant looked from bush to tree to rock and finally he saw a small dot. It was the mouse. He bent his head down so he could hear what the mouse was saying.

"Who do you think you are?" asked the mouse boldly. "Look at me. I am the master of this forest. What do you think of that?"

The elephant, aiming his trunk at the speck on the ground,

gushed forth all the water he had sucked up for his bath. *Whoosh!* The mouse was thrown ears over heels down the path with the sudden flood. He lay there for a moment, half dead from shock, and next door to drowned, besides.

When he came to his senses again, the elephant was gone. "What a storm that was!" exclaimed the mouse. "And it's a lucky thing for that elephant. If the sky hadn't opened up with a cloudburst, I would have broken the elephant to bits."

Home he went, singing to himself. When he arrived, there was his uncle waiting by the path to greet him. "And did you tell the elephant who was master of this forest?" asked his uncle, smiling behind his paw.

"I had just told him who was master of the forest when *Whoosh!* all the water in the sky came down in such a cloudburst that we were washed apart from one another. For all I know, he was drowned. I never saw him again. Better for him that he drowned rather than be broken to bits!"

Down he sat in his old corner. And if the elephant has not come along since to dispute him, he is still telling the same story.

Who's There? And What Do You Want?

Once there was and twice there wasn't a sensible black nanny goat. Her frisky billy goat husband had long since drowned in the river rushing past their house. So there she lived, with her two little kids, in a cave with a wooden door and one small window.

Every day the nanny goat went out into the forest to find food for their dinner. And every day before she went, she said the same thing. "Medik and Muduk, do *not* open the door to anyone but me. The wolf and the fox and the big black bear would all like to eat you. Beware of their tricks." And then off she would go.

"Pooh!" scoffed Muduk one day. "She says that every time. And here we stay, with no company at all but ourselves."

Suddenly, *Tok, tok, tok!* There came a knocking at the door. Medik looked at Muduk. Muduk looked at Medik. They began to shiver. Who could it be?

Then Muduk laughed. "What silly kids we are to be afraid! I am going to open the door." And he trotted toward the door.

"Wait, Muduk," said Medik. "Let me look out the window first." And he hurried to the window. By poking his head way out, he could just see the doorstep. And there stood the big black bear! Quickly he drew back his head. "It's the big black bear," he whispered. "What shall we do?"

"I'll take care of this," said Muduk. And, "Who's there?" he called, in a big bold voice. "And what do you want?"

"It is your mother," called the big black bear in his furry voice. "Open the door. I have brought you something to eat."

"You are not our mother," said Muduk. "Our mother has a

thin, sweet voice. You are the big black bear. Go away, black bear. We will not let you in."

"Hmn," thought the big black bear. "A thin, sweet voice . . ." and he hurried away home. He took out a tray of honeyed *baklava*, sweet, delicious baklava. He ate and ate, testing his voice every now and then. At last he was satisfied. Back he went to the nanny goat's house. *Tok, tok, tok!* he knocked. He took care to stand on the side of the door away from the window.

Medik ran to the window. He looked out as far as his neck could reach. But he could not see the black bear on the doorstep. Who could it be?

"Who is there?" called Muduk in a big bold voice. "And what do you want?"

"It is your mother," called the big black bear in a thin, sweet voice. "Open the door. I have brought you some food."

"Wait!" whispered Medik. "Our mother has red henna on her paws. Ask to see her paws."

"Our mother has beautiful paws," called Muduk. "Put your beautiful paws under the door so we may see them."

The big black bear slipped his paws under the door. Muduk began to laugh. "You are not our mother," he said. "Our mother has red henna on her paws. That is why they are so beautiful. Go away, big black bear. We will not let you in."

"Hmmn," thought the big black bear. "Henna on her paws . . ." and he hurried away home. He soaked and soaked his paws in a blood pudding he was making, until they were red, all red. Back he went to the nanny goat's house. *Tok, tok, tok!* he knocked. He took care to stand at the side of the door away from the window.

Medik ran to the window. He looked out as far as his neck could reach. But he could not see the big black bear on the doorstep. Who could it be?

"Who is there?" called Muduk in a big bold voice. "And what do you want?"

"It is your mother, children," called the big black bear, remembering to use his thin, sweet voice. And he slipped his red, red paws under the door. "Open the door. I have brought you some food."

"It *is* our mother!" said Muduk.

"No, it isn't," said Medik.

And so they began to quarrel.

Tok, tok, tok! There was that knocking at the door again. "Come, children," said the black bear in his thinnest, sweetest voice. "Please don't keep your mother waiting here on the doorstep."

"I'm going to open the door for Mother," said Muduk.

"And *I'm* going to hide in the sack of spoons," said Medik. And quickly he burrowed down among the spoons in the sack.

"Come in, Mother," said Muduk, and he unlocked the door. In rushed the big black bear.

Muduk began to run here and there, but the big black bear was too quick for him. *Ka-chomp!* With one swallow, Muduk was gone, down deep inside the big black bear. From inside the sack of spoons, Medik listened. He heard the big black bear tramping, tramping, looking for another little kid. But the big black bear never thought of the sack of spoons. At last he left, slamming the door behind him.

When he heard no more noise, Medik crept out of the sack. He hurried to lock the door again. He waited and waited. At last his mother came home. "Oh, Mother!" he cried, "the big black bear ate Muduk!" And he told his mother all about it.

Now, his mother was a very clever nanny goat. "Help me," she said, and together they lifted their big cellar door to a corner of the room. They covered the cellar opening with plenty of branches, until it looked like a nice, soft place to sit. "Wait here," she said. "I am going to bring the big black bear here for dinner. He will not hurt you when I am here." And off she went to find the big black bear.

"Neighbor bear!" she called. "You ate one of my naughty little kids. Come and I shall cook the other one for your dinner."

Now, in truth, the big black bear was still hungry. He came out of his cave and went along, went along, with the nanny goat. When he came to her house, sure enough, there was a huge caldron of water already boiling. He smacked his lips.

"Come inside and sit on that comfortable couch I have fixed for you," she said. "I shall pop my other little kid into the pot. Soon dinner will be ready. Meanwhile, we can talk."

The big black bear walked to the brushy branches and sat

down. *Ka-bloomp!* Down he went into the cellar! He began to bellow in pain and anger. Together, Medik and the nanny goat dragged the caldron of boiling water to the hole. They toppled it over onto the big black bear. The light went out of his eyes, and he was dead.

The nanny goat went outside and sharpened her horns. Then she came inside bringing a ladder and put it down into the hole. She climbed down carefully into the cellar. Rip, rip, rip, she ripped at the bear's stomach with her sharp horns until she had made a large hole. Suddenly, out stepped Muduk, alive and well, and much, much wiser now about bears.

Medik and Muduk and their clever nanny mother had bear steaks for dinner. And that particular bear never knocked at their door again.

Hasan, the Heroic Mouse-Child

Once there was and once there wasn't a man who had no child. Oh, he and his wife *wanted* a child, but none came. At last his wife prayed, "O Allah, send us a child, even if it be no bigger nor better than a mouse."

That day, the ears of Allah were open, and in good time the woman gave birth to a child. Nothing but a mouse he was, small and gray, with wise eyes and twitching whiskers. The neighbors were surprised, but the man and his wife were glad to have any child at all, and they named him Hasan.

As the child grew, he helped more and more around the house, and his parents rejoiced in their lively son.

One morning as the good woman was preparing a hot lunch for her husband, Hasan stood up tall on a stool. "See how big I am, my mother," he said. "Let me take the lunch to my father in the field."

"You *are* big, my dear," answered his mother, "but you are not quite big enough to manage our donkey while he carries the lunch to the field."

"Listen, my mother," said Hasan. "I can say 'Deh' and 'Chush' as well as the rest, and the donkey knows me well. If I am high on his back, the donkey will go and stop for me. I can ride in the saddlebag. You'll see!"

So Hasan's mother put the lunch in a tin box and tucked it into one pocket of the saddlebag, and she helped Hasan into the other pocket.

"*Deh!*" called the mouse-child, and off the donkey started for the field.

Hasan's father was surprised to see the donkey coming all by himself to the field. *"Aman!"* he exclaimed. But just as he was about to take to his heels with fear, *"Chush!"* shouted Hasan. And there stood Hasan, peeking over the edge of the saddlebag, with his bright eyes watching his father's surprise.

His father laughed and helped him down, and the two ate a good hot lunch together.

When it was time for his father to work again, the mouse-child scrambled up into the saddlebag. *"Deh!"* he shouted, and off went the donkey toward home.

On their way home, they came to the village fountain. *"Chush!"* shouted Hasan, and the donkey stopped. "You must be thirsty, my donkey," said the mouse-child. "Have a good drink while I climb to the top of that poplar tree. If I'm up high, I can see how the whole village looks!"

Leg over leg, Hasan climbed to the top of the tree. "Ah! Indeed I *can* see the whole village!" he said to himself.

Suddenly Hasan saw three men behind a bush near the fountain. They were counting: "One, two, three, one, two, three, one, two, three." And they were counting *gold coins*!

"Hmmnn!" said Hasan. "If they are hiding behind that bush, those may be stolen coins. I'll soon find out."

And boldly Hasan began to whistle the tune the village watchman whistled as he came down the street.

Startled, the three men looked this way and that, but they could not see the watchman. Frightened, they shoved the sack of gold coins into a hole under the bush. Then they ran out of the village as fast as they could go.

As soon as they had gone, Hasan scrambled down the poplar tree. "I can't lift that sack, but I *can* lift those coins one by one," he said.

And, one by one, Hasan carried the coins to the saddlebag of the donkey and dropped them, *Clink! Clink! Clink!*, into the pocket.

As soon as all of the coins were safe in the saddlebag, Hasan pushed the empty sack down deep, deep, deep, in that hole under the bush.

Then, climbing into the other pocket of the saddlebag, Hasan shouted *"Deh!"* and off the donkey trotted toward home.

9

"*Chush!*" called Hasan as the donkey came to Hasan's house, and the donkey stopped. Hasan's mother came to the door.

"Hasan!" she said. "I was afraid you were lost!"

Hasan laughed. "No, Mother. I was not lost. But I found something very useful. Come and see!" And he scrambled over to the other pocket of the saddlebag.

When his mother saw the gold coins, she could scarcely believe her eyes. And she was even more surprised when Hasan told her how he had frightened the robbers. "My mother," said Hasan, "even a mouse-child can make himself tall enough to help his parents."

It wasn't long before the man and his wife and the mouse-child were living in a fine new house. And, just for Hasan the hero, the house had a little balcony on top, so that Hasan could watch all the people come and go.

You see, you never can tell what will happen when you ask for a child no bigger nor better than a mouse!

The Magpie and the Milk

"There!" said the old lady as she finished milking her cow. "I'll leave the milk pail here while I go to fetch some sticks for my fire. Then I shall boil this fine fresh milk." And off she went.

While the old lady was gone, down flew a magpie. "Ah! Fresh milk!" said the magpie. "I'll just dip my beak in, and have some of that milk." But—oops!—over went the pail, and the milk was all spilled out. Just as the magpie was settling down to drink at a small puddle of milk, back came the old lady.

"Oh, you rascal!" exclaimed the old lady. She caught him by the tail.

The magpie tried so hard to fly away that his tail came off in the old lady's hand. "Old lady, old lady," said the magpie, "please give me back my tail."

"Yes, indeed," said the old lady, "just as soon as you bring me some more milk!"

The magpie thought for a minute. Then he hopped over to the cow. "Cow, cow. Please give me some milk for the old lady," he said. "Then she will give me back my tail."

"Yes, indeed," said the cow, "just as soon as you bring me some nice fresh grass."

The magpie thought for a minute. Then he hopped to a nearby field. "Field, field," he begged. "Please give me some nice fresh grass. I can give the grass to the cow and she will give me some milk. Then I can give the milk to the old lady and she will give me back my tail."

"Yes, indeed," said the field, "just as soon as you bring me some fresh, cool water."

The magpie thought for a minute. Then he hopped off to find a water carrier. "Water carrier, water carrier," he begged. "Please give me some fresh, cool water for the field. The field will then give me some nice fresh grass. I can give the grass to the cow and she will give me some milk. Then I can give the milk to the old lady and she will give me back my tail."

"Yes, indeed," answered the water carrier, "just as soon as you bring me a fine fresh egg for my lunch."

The magpie thought for a minute. Then he hopped off to find a hen. "Hen, hen," he begged. "Please give me a fine fresh egg. I can give the egg to the water carrier. Then he will give me some fresh, cool water. I can give the water to the field. Then the field will give me some nice fresh grass. I can give the grass to the cow and she will give me some milk. Then I can give the milk to the old lady and she will give me back my tail."

The hen thought for a minute. Then she said, "Since you are a bird and I am a bird, I will help you. Sit down and wait." The magpie sat and the hen sat. Suddenly the hen began to cluck. "There!" she said. She got up, and there was a fine fresh egg.

"Oh, *thank* you," said the magpie, and he took the egg to the water carrier. "Here is your fine fresh egg," he said. "Now may I have some fresh, cool water?"

"Ah, yes," answered the water carrier. "Here is your fresh, cool water."

"Oh, *thank* you," said the magpie, and he took the water to the field. "Here is your fresh, cool water," he said. "Now may I have some nice fresh grass?"

"Ah, yes," answered the field. "Here is your nice fresh grass."

"Oh, *thank* you," said the magpie, and he took the grass to the cow. "Here is your nice fresh grass," he said. "Now may I have some milk for the old lady?"

"Ah, yes," answered the cow. "Just milk me into that pail."

"Oh, *thank* you," said the magpie, and he filled the pail with foaming milk. Then he hopped to the old lady. "Come with me," he said. "I have a pail of milk for you. *Now* will you give me back my tail?"

"Yes, indeed," said the old lady, and she gave him back his tail. He fastened it on again and flew to join his friends.

As for the old lady, she settled down to boil her milk. Smell it?

The Mosquito and
the Water Buffalo

One day a tiny mosquito sat on the rough, thick-skinned neck of a water buffalo. Just then a car passed by, and the water buffalo was frightened and started running as fast as he could.

The poor mosquito, surprised at the extent of her might, came to the edge of the water buffalo's ear and said, "Brother Water Buffalo, I didn't mean to hurt you so much when I sat down. Please forgive me."

The Rabbit and the Wolf

One day when a rabbit was walking in the forest, he heard someone crying out, "Help! Help!" He looked around, and finally he saw a wolf. A great stone had fallen on his back so that he could not get up. He asked the rabbit's help, and said that he would die if nobody helped him.

The rabbit worked very hard, and finally managed to get the big stone off the wolf's back. Then the wolf jumped up and caught the rabbit in his mouth. The rabbit cried and asked for pity, but the wolf insisted on killing him for his meal.

Then the rabbit said, "No good person kills someone who has helped him. It is not fair. You can ask the duck, who is very fat and knows everything."

So both of them went to the duck. He listened to their story and then he said, "Show me the stone." They went to the stone.

"Now, let me be sure about this," said the duck. "Put the stone on the wolf's back exactly as it was when you found him." So the wolf lay down, and with much effort the stone was put on his back again.

"Well, what do you think?" said the wolf to the duck.

The duck thought for a moment. Then he said, "I think you were wrong to be cruel to the rabbit, who had helped you. Now see if someone else will help you!"

And leaving him in the sorry state in which the rabbit had come upon him, they went their way.

The Lion's Den

Once the lion, king of all the animals, assembled his subjects and asked them this question: "How does my den smell?"

After a timid silence, a dog spoke up. "Your Majesty," said the honest but unwise dog, "it smells rather unpleasant. In fact—forgive me, but it stinks!"

"How dare you!" roared the lion, and, springing upon the dog, he tore him to bits.

Then the lion repeated the question. This time an eager monkey ventured: "Sir, your honorable den smells like the very roses that bloom in palace gardens!"

"Oh?" said the lion. "Well, for this false flattery, you deserve the same treatment as the dog," and he destroyed the monkey, also.

The question was this time directed at the sly fox. "Your Majesty," replied the fox, "for some time now, I've had a bad cold, and I really can't tell . . ." and saved his precious life, of course.

The Crow and the Snake

There once was a crow who had a nest on a tree at the top of a mountain. Near her nest was the pit of a snake. Whenever the crow laid eggs, the snake would swallow them. The crow felt very sad about this situation. One day she described her plight to a jackal, and said:

"I want to tell you what I have decided about it. I want to peck the snake's eyes out and make him blind. This is the only way I can get rid of him."

The jackal replied, "The remedy that you suggest is a bad one. Find a remedy where you will not risk your own life, or else you will be like the fisher who tried to kill the lobster and was killed himself."

"How did this happen?" asked the crow.

And the jackal told this story:

"They say that there was once a marten who had settled at a place where there were many fish. He had lived there a long time and had become very old. As he was no longer able to fish, he was suffering from hunger. One day as he was sitting with his head in his paws and frowning, there came a lobster and looked at his sulky face and asked, 'Hey, marten, why are you so sorrowful?'

"The marten gave this answer: 'Why shouldn't I be sorrowful? Here I have earned my livelihood by fishing. But today two fishermen passed by here, and one said to the other, "There are many fish here. We had better fish here." The other one said, "I saw a great quantity of fish in another place. Let's start there, and come here afterward to catch the fish that are here.'' So I understand that after they have finished fishing at the other place they will come here and finish all the fish that are here. If they do so, I will die of hunger.'

"After listening to the marten, the lobster went and told the fish what he had heard. So all the fish came and asked the marten for advice: 'We came to ask advice from you because those who are intelligent ask for intelligence even from their enemies.'

"The marten replied, 'I cannot oppose the violence of the fishermen. I can tell you to go to a river where there is much water and reed. If you can only get there, then you and all your children and grandchildren will be saved.'

"The fish replied, 'We shall be happy to go if you will take us there.'

"So the marten agreed to take them to safety. Every day he took two fish along. But he took these fish only as far as a certain hill, where he ate them. This went on for some time.

"Then one day the lobster said, 'I am lonely and frightened here. Please take me to that river.'

"The marten agreed. When he and the lobster arrived at the hill where he had eaten the fish, the lobster saw the fishbones on the ground, thought of his faith, and said to himself: 'Whether a man wants to fight or not, when he knows that he will die and he meets his enemy, the thing he must do is to protect his honor and fight.' With these words he squeezed the marten's neck and killed him. After saving his own life, he went and told the rest of the fish what he had done."

The jackal said that he had told this story to show the crow that he must destroy a cheater by tricks.

"Let me tell you how to kill the snake without risking your own life."

"Yes," replied the crow. "What can I do?"

The jackal explained his plan: "Just fly around and watch carefully. Then take one of the precious jewels of a lady and fly away with the crowd watching you. Without disappearing from sight, take the jewel to the pit of the snake and leave it there. On seeing this, the crowd will kill the snake to recover the jewel. In this way you can get rid of the snake."

The crow, taking this advice, flew away, and from the roof of a house she saw a girl taking a bath, with her clothes and jewels laid aside. Immediately she swooped down and grabbing a jewel she flew away. Those who saw her grabbing the jewel started to run after her. The crow, without disappearing from the sight of her pursuers, flew to the pit of the snake and dropped the jewel there. On seeing this, the pursuers ran to the pit, killed the snake, and recovered the jewel.

Thus can intelligence defeat force and power.

Lazy Keloğlan and
the Sultan's Daughter

Once there was and once there wasn't a bald-headed boy called *Keloğlan*. Keloğlan was so lazy that he wouldn't lift a finger to help his poor widowed mother.

Finally his mother said, "Son, ride your donkey to the city, where you will see many people working. Perhaps there you will find a way to earn our bread and cheese."

"Mother," said Keloğlan, "you know how I am: When I'm *off* my donkey, I'm *off* my donkey; when I'm *on* my donkey, I'm *on* my donkey. To *get on* or *get off* is too much work."

But, "Go," said his mother firmly, "and may your way be open." Pushing him across the doorstep, she shut the door behind him. *Snick!* went the latch.

Grumbling, Keloğlan climbed on his donkey. He was too lazy to pick up the reins, but the donkey knew the road, so off they went toward the city, *cluf, cluf, cluf.*

As they came to a stream, Keloğlan saw a fish flopping about on the dusty bank. "Please put me back into the water, where I belong," said the fish.

Keloğlan said, "When I'm *on* my donkey, I'm *on* my donkey. To *get off* my donkey is too much work."

"Please," begged the fish, "put me back into the water."

"You *heard* me," said Keloğlan. "When I'm *on* my donkey, I'm *on* my donkey, and there I stay. It's just my way!"

The fish spoke a third time: "*Please* put me back into the water. Your bald head hides a clever wit. *Use* that wit."

Now, though Keloğlan was lazy—and stubborn, to boot—he *did* have the wit of every true bald one. Climbing down from his donkey, he picked up the fish with both hands and, *Luk!*, dropped it into the stream.

As Keloğlan was rinsing his hands, the fish raised his head above the water. "Here is a bit of magic for you," the fish said. "When you need something, say, 'For the sake of the fish, give me what I ask.' Then ask what you wish, and it will be granted." With that, the fish swam away.

Keloğlan dried his hands on his trousers. Then, shrugging his shoulders, he climbed onto his donkey, and along went the two toward the city.

As they entered the gate, Keloğlan saw all kinds of men— fat ones, thin ones, short ones, tall ones, ugly ones, handsome ones—hurrying toward the sultan's palace. Since that was the road *he* was taking, Keloğlan went along, too.

Now, the sultan had a daughter who was very beautiful except for one feature: her head had not a single hair on it. Her eyes were black as jet; her cheeks were rosy as ripe apples; her lips were redder than rubies. But, alas, her bald scalp undid all her beauty.

One after another, princes had come to woo her, but none could see her eyes or her cheeks or her lips for the shining of that bald head. Finally, her father had had enough of proud princes—in truth, he had almost had enough of his bald-headed daughter. "It seems *beauty* is *nothing,* yet *hair* is *everything,*" he exclaimed. "We shall see what my daughter's *fortune* can bring her, since her *face* has brought her nothing but disappointment."

He ordered all men interested in marrying the princess to gather beneath the princess's balcony on the next market day. "My daughter will throw a golden ball," he announced. "Whoever is hit by that golden ball will win both the princess and half of my kingdom."

Though no one was eager to win the princess, *everyone* wanted half of the sultan's kingdom, so men came flocking by tens and hundreds to the sultan's palace. Keloğlan, carried along by the crowd, came at last to the sultan's courtyard, beneath the princess's balcony.

As Allah would have it, the princess's ball landed with a *Tuk!* squarely on Keloğlan's bald head.

Seeing this, the sultan cried, "*One* bald head is one too

21

many. *Two* bald heads would be *two* too many! Here, daughter. Throw another ball."

Aiming carefully, the princess threw the second ball, and, *Tuk!*, it landed precisely on Keloğlan's shiny head.

"The chances of a Turk are *three*," said the sultan gruffly. "Aim carefully, my daughter. This next ball will be your last." And he handed her a third golden ball.

"I begin with the name of Allah!" murmured the princess. With exceeding care, she threw the third ball. *Tuk!* It landed exactly in the middle of Keloğlan's shiny scalp.

"Bald or not, he must be your husband," sighed the sultan. At once, he sent his chief vizier to fetch Keloğlan.

"Come, young man," said the vizier. "Leave your donkey and follow me."

Keloğlan shook his head. "When I'm *on* my donkey, I'm *on* my donkey, and not even for a princess will I get down. That's just my way," said he.

But the vizier pulled him off the donkey. "Come at once and claim your bride," he said, "*and* half of the sultan's kingdom, into the bargain!" He led Keloğlan directly to the sultan's audience chamber.

Suddenly, there stood Keloğlan, face to face with the scowling sultan and his sad-eyed, bald-headed daughter. Keloğlan, knowing better than most the nimble wit that lay beneath the princess's shiny pate, rejoiced that he had heeded the fish's plea.

"For the sake of the fish," he said, "give me what I ask: May the sultan's daughter have beautiful thick black hair flowing clear to her waist."

As Keloğlan finished speaking, the princess felt a strange prickling in her scalp, and, true enough, there it came—black, beautiful, long hair. Her eyes sparkled; her cheeks glowed; her lips smiled as they had never smiled before. The whole court stared, unable to believe what they saw.

As for the princess, she had eyes only for her Keloğlan. They were soon married, in a wedding that lasted forty days and forty nights, and for all I know, they are married yet, with more than enough bread and cheese for them and for Keloğlan's mother, besides. May we have a share of their good fortune!

The Three Brothers
and the Hand of Fate

Once there was and twice there wasn't, when *jinns* played polo in the old Turkish bath—well, in those days there was a farm family with three sons. Time came, time went, and first the old wife died, and then her husband died of sorrow.

"Now there are only three of us left," said the oldest son. "We have our father's barns and his livestock. We can divide those, and each of us can make the best of what fate sends him."

"Yes," said the middle son. "Each of us will choose one of our father's three barns. Tonight, when the livestock come home from pasture, we'll let each creature choose the barn he wishes."

The third son, Keloğlan, added, "In that event, each of our fortunes will be set by the hand of fate. That seems fair enough."

"Since we have agreed on that plan," said the oldest, "now we'll each choose a barn. As the first son, I'll take the newest, largest barn."

"And I," said the middle son, "will take the smaller new barn."

As for Keloğlan, he was left with the shed that had been built before he was in his cradle—small, shabby, but large enough, it seemed. For when they came home from pasture, only the poorest, weakest animals stumbled their way to Keloğlan's shed. The better, stronger animals chose one or the other of the newer, larger barns. "Well, that's fate, and fair enough, as you said, Keloğlan," said the eldest. And he and the middle one had reason indeed to be satisfied.

Keloğlan swallowed his disappointment. But three or five days later, he took all of his animals to sell in a village some distance from the farm. By the time he had sold all his animals for the best price he could get, there was little daylight left. Keloğlan tucked the money from his day's business into his wide sash and started home.

"Since it is almost dark," said Keloğlan, "I'll spend the night somewhere along the way. I can go the rest of the way home after dawn." The only place he could find to stay was a deserted grain mill some distance from the road. "I'll stay there," he decided. "It's better than no shelter at all." Inside, he found a large grain bin, and he settled himself there to sleep.

As he slept, he dreamed he heard voices—voices not of men but of jinns. But as the voices grew louder, he half wakened and looked cautiously over the edge of the bin. He *hadn't* dreamed it! There were seven jinns, each bigger than the other and more ugly, gathered about a huge dining tray, talking and drinking and enjoying a fine feast. Keloğlan listened.

One jinn said, "In the land beyond the seven mountains there is a *padişah* whose only son is blind. For three or five years, the padişah and his people have searched in vain for a cure for the prince's blindness. Only *I* know a cure. On the edge of the next village along this very road there is a stunted poplar tree whose leaves hold a powerful medicine. If the prince's eyes were rubbed with leaves from that poplar tree, he would see as clearly as a mirror!"

A second jinn said, "Seeing is all very well, but what do you say to *treasure*, mounds and mounds of it? The richest treasure hoard in all this land is buried in the small hill that rises from the long valley between the two rivers. I'm the only one who knows exactly where in the hill that gold is buried!"

Not to be outdone, a third jinn said, "To restore sight is splendid, and to find gold makes one wealthy, but to supply water to a whole village is to create a miracle. There is a village between here and the land beyond the seven mountains that has no water at all. Daily, the women must walk twenty kilometers to the next village to get the water for their families. But I—and only I—know that there is a spring of fresh water under the walnut tree near the mosque. Beneath the main root of that walnut tree, a huge rock has become wedged, and it blocks the passage of the spring. If that rock were removed, the whole village would have water a-plenty."

Just as the third jinn had finished speaking, a cock crowed, and, quicker than it takes to say so, the jinns disappeared, leaving nothing but the scraps of their feast behind them. Keloğlan ate the last of the scraps to fill his hungry stomach for the work he had in mind.

Quietly, quietly, then, he left the mill and began to walk down the road toward the village where the stunted poplar grew. Keloğlan went right past the farm where his brothers were still sleeping, with their fine, strong livestock in their new barns. Putting one foot after the other in the cool morning light, he came to the next village. True enough, there was the stunted poplar tree, and he gathered a good supply of the leaves to tuck into his sash.

The village market had barely begun to do business. As for Keloğlan, he had business there himself. "The journey to the land beyond the seven mountains is a long one," he told himself, "and I shall need a horse for that journey. Besides, who knows how long these poplar leaves will hold their power? I must go quickly." Using most of the money in his sash, Keloğlan drove a good bargain for a strong horse, and, *chick-a-dock, chick-a-dock, chick-a-dock,* he rode and rode, until finally he came to the land he was seeking.

At once, he went to the palace of the padişah. As soon as he had told the servants his errand, they took him to the padişah. "My padişah," he said, "I have brought a cure for the prince's blindness."

"My son," said the padişah, "many people have brought cures for my son's blindness, but none of them has healed him. Still, *welcome*, anyway. If you *do* restore my son's sight, I shall reward you richly."

Keloğlan was taken immediately to the prince's room. "*Bismillah!*" murmured Keloğlan as he took the poplar leaves from his sash and rubbed them firmly on the prince's eyes. Then he waited and watched. And the padişah watched with him.

Suddenly, "Father! Father! I see a little light!" cried the prince. And then, little by little, his vision became clearer and brighter, until he could see as well as anyone else.

"Thank you! Thank you!" cried the padişah, weeping with

joy and relief. "Now, ask whatever you will, and it shall be granted."

"I wish only your good health," said Keloğlan.

"No, no!" the padişah insisted. "My health is my own concern. Ask something for *yourself*."

"Well, then, my padişah, I should be happy to have forty strong mules and forty strong laborers for forty days' time. No later than the end of the forty days, I shall return the mules and the laborers to you."

"You shall have what you ask," declared the padişah, "and supplies for you and the men and the mules for forty days, besides!" And he ordered the mules well loaded for whatever use Keloğlan wished to make of them.

With each laborer riding a mule and Keloğlan riding his horse, they came in three or five days to the waterless village. Keloğlan went to the *muhtar* of the village and said, "I have come to provide water for your thirsty villagers. I ask only that my laborers be allowed to dig under the walnut tree at the center of the village."

"Dig away, my son," said the muhtar. "We *are* thirsty in this village. If you can indeed provide us with water, we shall provide you with a fine new house and a stable for your horse, and with our thanks forever."

Keloğlan set the laborers to work digging under the walnut tree, carefully, carefully, so as not to destroy the tree. True enough, after several days of digging, they found the huge rock that blocked the spring, and they brought it to the surface. That rock is still there, at the base of the fountain built where the spring began to flow strongly and sweetly.

Then, true to his word, the muhtar set his own laborers to work building Keloğlan's fine house and stable. As for Keloğlan and his forty laborers, they had further work to do. They rode and rode until they came to the long valley between two rivers. "Do you see that small hill?" asked Keloğlan. "Dig here and there in that hill for the treasure that is buried there."

The laborers began to dig, some here, some there, until "Here it is!" shouted one, and they all hurried over to dig in that spot. There they found many large earthenware jars just *filled* with gold coins. The coins were loaded into the mules' saddlebags, by now almost empty of supplies for the forty days. Then the forty mules, the forty laborers, and Keloğlan went to Keloğlan's old home.

"What do you have in those saddlebags?" asked his oldest brother as Keloğlan halted before the door.

"It might be the red gold wheat that the hand of fate has provided," said Keloğlan, smiling.

"Let me see it," said the second brother, and he ran his hands through the "wheat." "Wheat!" he exclaimed. "That's not *wheat*; that's gold!"

"So it is," said Keloğlan, "and you can each get as much treasure as that for yourselves." And he told them exactly what he had done to learn the jinns' secrets. "Be patient, my brothers, and you, too, can become rich. As for me, I must be on my way beyond the seven mountains to return the mules and these laborers to the padişah." And off he went with his caravan, stopping only long enough at his new house to unload the gold from thirty-nine of the saddlebags and hide it safely.

On the thirty-ninth day, he came into the presence of the padişah of that other land. "My padişah," he said, "I have completed the work I planned, and I have been well satisfied with the laborers you let me use. Here is a saddlebag of gold pieces that you may divide as you wish among the men. I beg your permission now to return to my own home."

"Go, my son," said the padişah, "and may your way be open." Thus it was that Keloğlan had both his needs and his wishes fulfilled at the hand of fate.

As for Keloğlan's brothers, they went to the old mill night after night after night, for six nights, and hid in two of the grain bins, but no jinns came. On the seventh morning, the oldest brother said bitterly, "What a poor piece of nonsense this has been! That Keloğlan has made fools of us both!"

But the middle brother said, "Remember, my brother, what Keloğlan said: 'Be patient.' Let us try again, one more night. If the jinns do not come tonight, we may well seek out Keloğlan and persuade him to share his wealth with us."

That seventh night, then, they hid themselves in the same grain bins in the old mill, and waited, and waited . . . As Allah would have it, that night the jinns *did* come, and they feasted and drank and talked. But their talk was of quite another temper from what Keloğlan had heard.

The first jinn said, "Someone must have been hiding somewhere in the mill the last time we met here, and listened as we talked. I have heard that the son of the padişah of the land beyond the seven mountains is no longer blind, but sees as well as anyone else."

"Aha!" said the third jinn, "and I have heard that the waterless village now has a spring with a rock at the base of the fountain exactly like the one that had stopped the spring at the root of the walnut tree."

"Alas!" said the second jinn, "that treasure in the small hill is gone, too—all gone. There is no sign of it at all."

"Let's look right now, before we tell any more of our secrets, to see whether someone might be hiding here tonight," said the sixth jinn. So all seven of the jinns looked everywhere in the mill, and at last they found the two brothers in the grain bins. They took the brothers out, both half dead from fear.

"We'll open the sluices to start the millstones turning," said the fifth jinn, "and we'll hold their heads against the millstones until their ears are all worn off. *Then* let them try to hear the secrets that jinns tell!"

Just as the older brother's right ear was being held to the rolling millstone, a cock crowed, and, quicker than it takes to say so, the jinns had disappeared.

The two brothers stared at one another. Then each one felt his ears. Yes, they were still there, two on each head. "I don't know about you, my brother," said the eldest, "but after the night's adventure I want no gold nor anything else from jinns. I'll take my own good ears and go home to my livestock."

"And I, too, brother," said the middle one. "What our father left us is fortune enough for me. Let us go home to what we know, and leave to Keloğlan whatever comes his way at the hand of fate."

So it was that Keloğlan's two older brothers kept both their ears and the family farm, while Keloğlan lived in comfort with the good will of his new neighbors and water enough to refresh them all. It's good water, too. I had some to drink when I was in that village not long ago.

Keloğlan and the
Twelve Dancing Princesses

Once there was and once there wasn't, long ago, when the camel was a barber and the flea a porter—well, in those times, there was a padişah who had twelve daughters, each one more beautiful than the one before her. All the princesses slept in the same large room, in beds as like as peas. And every night after the princesses had tucked themselves into their beds, their faithful old nurse would come and lock the door so there would be neither out nor in for them.

But one morning when the old nurse unlocked the door, she found the princesses' dancing shoes beneath their beds and worn right through the soles with dancing. Saying nothing to the princesses, she quietly inspected all the windows in the room, but every one was securely locked. Puzzled, but keeping her own counsel, she replaced the worn shoes with new ones.

The next morning when she came to unlock the princesses' door, she found the new dancing shoes in the same sorry state as the others. Surely, the princesses could not have been dancing in their own room, else the shoes would not have been worn to tatters . . . Well, this was a matter for the palace guards.

Here and there she went, inquiring, but none had seen the princesses leave the palace, though watch had been kept the night through. There remained but one choice: she must tell the padişah.

After counseling with his viziers about the matter, the padişah called the messengers of the palace to him. "My daughters," he announced, "leave the palace secretly each evening. Where they go, I know not; I know only that they go, and that they return after an evening of dancing. Where do they go, and what business are they about? The person who can bring me the answer to this question will be given as his bride whichever of my daughters he chooses. But any person who seeks the answer and *fails* will lose his head for his efforts! Go, now, and proclaim this message throughout my kingdom."

Almost on the heels of the messengers came scores of handsome young men to try for the hand of a princess. Each one who applied was allowed three nights to find the answer to the padişah's question. He was placed in a small room adjoining the princesses' bedroom so that he might watch and report what he saw. But night after night the luckless young men fell asleep and failed to note what happened. Morning after morning dawned on twelve worn pairs of dancing slippers, and every three days another handsome young man paid with his head for his failure.

One day young Keloğlan heard about the strange story of the padişah's twelve dancing daughters, and he resolved to try his fortune in the matter. "My bald head has always been a burden to me," he said to himself. "If I lose it, I lose it. On the other hand, if I *should* win the hand of a princess, who knows? I might some day cover my hairless head with a crown!" So saying, he set off for the padişah's palace. He walked a little, he walked far, picking hyacinths all the way.

One day in his travels he met a wrinkled old woman, and, "Good day, mother," said he.

"Good day, son," she answered. "And where might you be going?"

"Well, if you want the truth, I scarcely know myself, mother," he answered. "It seems there is a padişah with twelve dancing daughters. Allah willing, I shall find out where they dance. If Allah prosper me not, in three days I shall lose my head for my much trying. In either case, I shall benefit: Either I shall lose my bald head, which has always been a source of much trouble to me, or I shall gain the hand of a beautiful princess. What will be will be. I can but try."

"Ah, my son," said the old woman, "be not in such haste to throw away your young life! Listen carefully to me. When you are put into the small room next to the princesses, take care that you stay awake. Whatever potion they give to you will be a sleepy drink; do not so much as *taste* of it. And take this magic cloak with you. Whenever you wear it, no one at all can see you. And may Allah make a straight path before you!" The old woman patted Keloğlan on the shoulder, but when he turned to thank her, she had disappeared entirely.

On he went, one foot after the other, until he came at last to the padişah's palace. Now, the suitors had dwindled to none at all—for what man, however brave, would care to risk his life in such a bootless venture?—and the padişah was happy indeed to see even Keloğlan. In due time, the young man was taken to the small room next to the princesses' bedroom. As the old woman had advised, he took care not to drink the potion offered by the eldest princess. Oh, he accepted it willingly enough, but he used it after her departure to water the little crack in the tile behind his bed. Then, as if he had been overcome by the drug, he lay down on the bed and within the space of a few minutes busied himself with snoring. How they laughed, the padişah's twelve daughters!

"This one is even more stupid than the rest," exclaimed the eldest princess. "See him there, asleep—a *fine* watchman, he!" And the girls chattered freely among themselves as they dressed in their ball gowns—all but the youngest princess, who felt for some reason uneasy.

"I *do* hope nothing happens tonight," the youngest one sighed. "Somehow, I fear for us."

"Ah, there!" chaffed one of her sisters. "You have always been the timid one. Surely that foolish Keloğlan can do no harm. Come! Fasten your slippers, for we must go."

Tap! Tap! The eldest princess tapped slowly on the carpet. Suddenly in the middle of the floor a trapdoor yawned open, with a stairway going down from it. One by one the princesses descended the stairs, with Keloğlan right behind, wearing his magic cloak. As he came to the foot of the stairs, the boy wondered: *Was* the cloak truly magic? Or could the princesses see him? To test the matter, he stepped on the skirt of the youngest princess, who turned around and stared behind her in alarm. "Who stepped on my skirt?" she cried. "*Someone* is following us." Immediately, the other princesses looked, but there was no one in sight besides themselves.

"Ah, now," chided the eldest princess, "are you going to

spoil our evening with your worries? As you can see, there is no one behind you. You must have caught your hem upon a nail. Come along, now. We shall be late!"

They walked and walked, with Keloğlan at the heels of the youngest princess. Through bowers and along shaded roads they went, till they came to a forest of trees bent quite double with silver branches. "Oh," thought Keloğlan, "I *must* have one of those beautiful branches! I have seen nothing like them in the padişah's kingdom." And, *snap*, he broke a branch from the nearest tree and slipped it beneath his cloak in the folds of his wide sash.

Hearing the sound, the youngest princess turned pale. "What was that? I heard a noise!" she cried. "*Someone* is following us."

Again the eldest sister answered, "Come, now. Don't be afraid. Think only of the lovely evening we shall have."

Through a woods where the trees had leaves of gold, and through another woods where the trees had leaves bearing diamonds and pearls, they hurried. Keloğlan, reaching out in passing, plucked a twig carrying several gemmed leaves. *SNAP!* He quickly tucked the twig into his wide sash.

"Girls! Did you hear that noise?" called the youngest princess. But by that time, her sisters were too far ahead to be concerned by her cries. There at the shore of a velvet-black lake they were awaited by twelve handsome princes, each in his own canoe. One by one, the princesses were safely seated, with Keloğlan stepping into the canoe carrying the youngest princess.

To the surprise of the young prince, no matter how hard he paddled, he could not catch up with the others. "My darling," he said at last, "there is something strange about this canoe tonight. Why is it going so slowly?"

"Perhaps you are tired, my prince," answered the youngest princess. But, in truth, a chill wind of doubt and fear blew within her. This was altogether too strange a night.

Suddenly a broad band of light made a path along the water. Lanterns by the thousands gleamed in the palace on the opposite shore of the lake, and the sound of music drifted across the waves. Paddling with renewed strength, the young prince at last gained the far shore. Then he and the youngest princess (and

Keloğlan in his magic cloak) stepped out upon the beach, joining those from the other canoes. Together they entered the great ballroom, where they danced all evening to such engaging music that Keloğlan danced, too, all by himself, in a corner sparkling with lights and mirrors.

Presently a great banquet was ready, with the food served on silver plates and the drink in golden cups. Just as the first toast had been proposed, the youngest princess was surprised to find her golden cup quite empty. "Why," said she, "what happened to my drink? I hadn't even touched the cup. Someone drank from it!"

"Oh, you silly girl!" laughed her eldest sister. "You were warm from dancing, and you drank without even noticing." And they all teased her so that she said no more.

At last the dancing and the feasting came to an end, and the princes returned the padişah's daughters to the other side of the lake. As for Keloğlan, as soon as the canoe carrying the youngest princess had touched the shore, he leaped out and hurried ahead of the girls to the small room where he was to sleep. Lying down upon the bed, he began to snore softly.

Not long afterwards, the princesses arrived, and the eldest one immediately came to the door of the small room and laid her ear against it. "There is your dangerous Keloğlan!" she said mockingly to her youngest sister. "Hear him snore! Now tell me there was something strange about tonight."

Of course, what could the youngest say? She undressed with the rest, and soon they were all sound asleep.

The next day, Keloğlan said nothing at all of what he had seen. And that evening, he followed the princesses again to the palace across the lake, returning just ahead of them to the small room. The third night, too, he went with the princesses, this time bringing back the youngest princess's golden cup, tucked safely in the folds of the wide sash beneath his magic cloak.

As soon as Keloğlan had breakfasted the fourth morning, he and the twelve princesses were summoned to appear before the padişah. "Well, now, young man," said the padişah, "what can you tell us? What have you seen? Where is it that my daughters go each night to dance out the soles of their shoes?"

Without a moment's hesitation, Keloğlan replied, "I saw

your daughters, sire, dancing with twelve young, handsome princes."

Gravely the padişah addressed his daughters. "And what do *you* have to say to this, my dears?"

"Ridiculous!" sputtered the eldest princess. "He lay snoring in his room all three evenings. How can he pretend to have seen anything?"

"Hmn," mused the padişah. "Tell us more, young man. How can we be sure of what you say?"

Reaching inside the folds of his wide sash, Keloğlan drew forth the silver branch, the twig bearing leaves gemmed with diamonds and pearls, and the golden cup. The princesses sighed with one breath. But what could they say?

Then Keloğlan told the whole story, from first to last, leaving out not a single detail or a particle of conversation. And the flushed cheeks of the princesses gave the stamp of truth to all he said.

"You have brought the answer to my question, young man," said the padişah as Keloğlan's tale was finished. "Now all that remains is for you to choose one of my daughters as your bride. Which one will you have?"

"The youngest one," responded Keloğlan. "She is not only the cleverest, but also the most beautiful of all."

Thus it was that he married the padişah's youngest daughter, who, in truth, was half in love with him already. For forty days and forty nights a splendid wedding was celebrated, and the two lived happily ever after.

A story for them, I say,
And health for us.

Riddles

Big as an elephant, light as a bird. What is it?
(*The elephant's shadow*)

Little, little rooms, like as twin to brother,
Running, running, running after one another.
(*Train*)

Tiny little barrel hides
Pickles in its small insides.
(*Lemon*)

I Know What *I'll* Do

One day the *Hoca* fell asleep as he was jogging along the road on his little gray donkey. Seeing a fine chance for a joke, several of his students slipped up behind him and removed the worn saddlebag from his donkey's back. Then they waited to see what would happen.

When he arrived at his stable door, the Hoca dismounted and reached out to remove the saddlebag. To his astonishment, it had disappeared entirely. The Hoca rubbed his eyes and looked again, but the saddlebag was nowhere to be seen.

The next day he encountered several of his students on the street that ran past the public fountain. "Boys," said he, "my saddlebag is gone. If you don't bring it back to me, I know what *I'll* do . . ." and he muttered something under his breath.

The boys looked at one another in dismay. Their prank had suddenly become a serious matter. In no time at all, they brought the missing saddlebag and presented it to the Hoca.

Thanking them, the Hoca installed it in its rightful place on the back of his little donkey, and he was about to ride away when one of the boys could contain his curiosity no longer. "I say, Hoca *effendi*," he began, "what were you going to do if we did not return the saddlebag?"

"Ah," answered the Hoca mildly, "I have at home a piece of old carpet. If you had not returned the saddlebag, I should have had to make another one."

Nasreddin Hoca,
Seller of Wisdom

Once there lived in the Turkish town of Akşehir a stout little Muslim preacher called Nasreddin Hoca. For many years, the Hoca had freely given both help and good advice to the people of Akşehir, and he was loved and admired in fair return.

One day Nasreddin Hoca's wife went to a *hamam* in their town to have a good bath and a pleasant time for herself. Just as she was sitting down by a marble washbasin, however, the bath attendant came along and said, "No, no, not there, my lady. Move along to another basin, please. The wife of the merchant Hasan is going to wash here."

Quite cheerfully, the Hoca's wife gathered together her bath dipper and her soap and her comb and her towels and moved along to the next cubicle. No sooner had she seated herself there when along came the bath attendant again. "No, no, not there, my lady," the attendant said. "Please move to another basin, for the wife of the merchant Ahmet wants to wash here."

A bit annoyed but still good-natured, the Hoca's wife patiently gathered up her belongings and went along to the very last cubicle. She was just beginning to run warm water into the basin when there came that same bath attendant. "I am sorry, my lady, but you cannot use this basin, either. Merchant Mehmet's daughter plans to wash here. As you know, she is having her wedding bath today."

Looking about her and finding every other basin taken, the Hoca's wife realized that she would not be able to have her bath at all. Tying up her bath dipper and her comb and her soap and her clean towels snugly in her *bohça*, she went along home. "Merchants, merchants!'' she grumbled. ''It seems that nowadays the only man of consequence is a *merchant*.''

That evening before dinner, Nasreddin Hoca came into the house full of his usual good cheer. He was just about to ask his wife what gossip she had heard at the bath when he noticed her face. Indeed, it was as sour-looking as if she had spent the whole day at sucking lemons. He had not long to wait before he learned the cause of her bad temper.

''Merchant Hasan's wife and Merchant Ahmet's wife and even Merchant Mehmet's daughter had baths today, but not so much as a single basin could be spared for me!'' she sputtered. ''We have come to a pretty pass when merchants wag the town. But since that is the way matters stand, I have made up my mind. You must become a merchant.''

''A merchant!'' Nasreddin Hoca exclaimed. ''My dear wife, you know very well that one cannot say, 'I am a merchant' and by the saying become a merchant. One must have his pockets full and running over with good gold liras before he can so much as think of becoming a merchant. And look at *my* pockets!'' One after another, the Hoca turned his patched pockets inside out, revealing not so much as a single *kuruş*.

''Liras or no liras,'' responded his wife, ''you must become a merchant tomorrow or I'll—I'll leave you, and take the cow right along with me.''

''My dear,'' the Hoca said patiently, ''I can do very well without the cow, but I cannot get along without you. After all, you are the finest cook in Akşehir.''

But his wife was not to be flattered, it seems. ''You cannot have me, cook or no, unless you become a merchant,'' she insisted, her jaw set and her eye firm.

Remembering that the devil takes a hand in what is done in haste, the Hoca said agreeably, ''Very well, my good wife, but give me twenty-four hours to think how this business may be managed. With Allah's help, I shall surely find a way out of this thorny problem.''

That night, the Hoca tossed restlessly upon his straw mat, but no matter how long and how hard he thought, he was unable to see a means of setting himself up as a merchant. Nor could he find an answer to his dilemma during the long, hot day that followed.

But jogging homeward from his vineyard that afternoon on his little gray donkey, the Hoca suddenly had an idea. He could sell his beloved donkey and thereby raise enough money to rent a stall for a month or so in the marketplace. Riding on past his house to the market, the Hoca found a man willing to bargain with him for his donkey, and after much haggling he exchanged his donkey for twenty gold liras, exactly enough to rent a shop for a month.

That night, Nasreddin Hoca's wife came to the door to greet him. "Well, my dear," she said firmly, "you have had your twenty-four hours. Will you become a merchant?"

In answer, the Hoca pulled out his worn purse and showed his wife the twenty gold liras. "There, you see!" he said triumphantly. "I sold my donkey today, and I have the money to open a shop."

"What will you sell?" asked his wife as they walked on into the house.

"Only the good Allah knows," answered the Hoca. "I can buy no merchandise, for it will cost me all twenty liras for my rent. But I'll think of *something* to sell, my dear."

The next morning, Nasreddin Hoca went to find a shop, and once he had rented it, he entered into business as confidently as did all the other merchants. And his wife went to the bath and bathed at any of the basins she wished, just as did the wives of the other merchants.

There was only one difference between Nasreddin Hoca and the other merchants: they had shirts or towels or carpets or copper pots in their shops for the customers who came to buy, while the Hoca had in his shop nothing but one big earthen pot over in the far corner. Nevertheless, he rolled up the shutters of his shop each morning with exactly the right show of importance, and pulled the shutters down at night with exactly as sound a thump as the rest.

Day after day he sat in his empty shop, nodding at passersby and exchanging bits of news about this and that. People smiled behind their hands to see their Hoca selling nothing at all in the marketplace, but they had grown so used to his quirks by these years of knowing him that they were certain he had his reasons for what he was doing. And so he had: not once did his wife have cause to complain about her treatment at the hamam. And, after all, it was pleasant to do business of any sort at all in the marketplace.

One Friday just before noon, Nasreddin Hoca was seated as usual on a stool in his shop when with great ceremony the mighty Tamerlane passed by on his way to the mosque for the holy service. Seeing that the Hoca had apparently nothing at all to sell, Tamerlane stopped for a moment. "What is this!" he exclaimed. "You have a stall in the marketplace, my clever Hoca, yet you have no goods to sell."

Nasreddin Hoca, seldom at a loss for an answer, responded quickly, "Ah, but what greater good is there than wisdom, Your Majesty? It is *wisdom* I have to sell!" And he gestured toward the earthen pot in the corner.

"So your stock in trade is wisdom, eh?" mused the ruler. "How do you sell it?"

"One bit of wisdom is worth one gold lira," answered the Hoca.

"All right, then," agreed Tamerlane. "Sell me one lira's worth of wisdom." And he gave the Hoca a gold coin.

The Hoca thought for a moment. Then he said soberly, "This is the bit of wisdom I give you in exchange for your lira: 'Do not do anything without first considering its end.'"

"Ha!" said Tamerlane. "That seems scarcely worth a gold lira."

"Ah, but it is, Your Majesty," said the Hoca. "It is worth far more than a single gold lira. You will realize its value in days to come. Here. I shall write it out for you so that you may keep it ever near you." And going to the earthen pot, he drew forth a scroll. Taking his pen and inkhorn from his ample sash, he inscribed the wise saying in a large and flowing script and handed the parchment to Tamerlane. Rolling up the scroll and giving it to an attendant, Tamerlane nodded and went on his way to the mosque. As for the Hoca, he fingered the gold lira and reflected that business was, after all, worth a man's time and attention.

Now, it happened that at that time, Tamerlane's viziers were engaged in a plot to assassinate him. Wearied of his changeable moods and sudden decisions, they had determined to take his life and to set in his place a ruler more to their liking. After much thought and discussion, they had agreed that Tamerlane's personal barber would be the one best able to do the bloody deed for them. "Only cut his throat, and we shall make you the grand vizier," they promised, and thus they persuaded him to play the part of the assassin.

The following day, Tamerlane summoned his barber to give him his morning shave. In the room where Tamerlane received such visitors, he had framed and hung on the wall the wise statement which Nasreddin Hoca had sold him. Liking the bit of wisdom very well, he had begun the practice of reading it aloud before he made any decision or undertook any action. Therefore, just as the barber, his hand trembling, lifted the razor to his throat, intending to do the deed at once and have it over with, Tamerlane read aloud the saying, "Do not do anything without first considering its end."

The barber, already anxious indeed about the danger of the act he was committing, thought that Tamerlane was speaking directly to him. Terrified, he dropped his razor and fell to the floor at Tamerlane's feet. "Your Majesty, it is not my fault!" he babbled. "I was directed by your viziers to do this terrible thing. They told me to cut your throat, never dreaming that you would know about it."

Tamerlane, astounded by the barber's confession, sent at once for the conspirators and had them suitably punished. As soon as that business had been completed, he sent for Nasreddin Hoca. The Hoca, perplexed by this sudden summons, closed up his shop and hurried to the ruler's quarters.

As soon as Nasreddin Hoca had appeared before him, Tamerlane said, "In truth, Hoca, the wisdom that you sold me was worth far more than the gold lira you asked. As a matter of fact, it saved my life today."

Then, turning to his attendants, he said, "Give the Hoca this purse of gold. And take note of this order: For his services,

Nasreddin Hoca is to be made director of this whole province. Such a wise man deserves high position in my empire."

Thus it was that Nasreddin Hoca, seller of wisdom, harvested a rich return indeed from his venture as a merchant.

Nasreddin Hoca
and the Third Shot

One day as Nasreddin Hoca was chatting with the Emperor Tamerlane, he chanced to see archers practicing in a nearby field. "Ha! So *those* are your archers!" he exclaimed. And a reminiscent gleam came into his eye. "Not an archer in that whole field can shoot as well as I," he boasted. "In my youth, I was champion archer of this whole area of Turkey."

"Hmm," murmured Tamerlane. "Champion, eh? Well, if you were champion, you can certainly teach my men something. Come along. I was just about to ride out and inspect the practice."

At this, the Hoca began to tremble. In truth, he was no archer at all, and never had been. But to boast before the great Tamerlane and then fail to make good on one's boast could be a very expensive mistake. Deeply regretting his rash statement, the Hoca mounted his little gray donkey and trotted out after the Emperor to the field.

Calling his men to him, Tamerlane bade them attend closely, for they were to receive an archery lesson from a real champion. The Hoca was then given a bow and three arrows, and motioned to position.

In an effort to gain time, the Hoca gravely studied the target. By Allah, he could barely *see* it! He shook his head thoughtfully. "If I had only remembered to practice what I so often preach to my students: 'Listen a hundred times; ponder a thousand times; speak once'!" he mourned.

But Tamerlane was becoming impatient, and well the Hoca knew the cost of further delay. He could do no more than try . . . Taking careful aim, the Hoca released the first arrow. It wavered, and fell just a short distance ahead of him. The Hoca smiled confidently. *"That*, sire, is the way your captains shoot."

With even greater care, the Hoca placed and aimed the second arrow. Alas, it traveled very little farther than the first one. Here and there among the archers a chuckle was heard, speedily silenced by the baleful glance of Tamerlane. But the Hoca beamed, and proclaimed, *"That*, sire, is how your generals shoot."

With infinite care, the Hoca fitted the third arrow to the string. Calmly he spat to ward off the evil eye. Then he aimed the arrow. Allah help him, the bow slipped in his trembling hand, and the arrow, released with surprising force, flew straight to its goal, lodging itself neatly exactly in the center of the target.

The Hoca, much cleverer with his wits than with his hands, looked about him proudly. "And *that*, sire, is how your humble servant Nasreddin Hoca used to shoot when he was archery champion!"

The Hoca as
Tamerlane's Tax Collector

One day the Hoca chanced to be in Tamerlane's court when the despot's tax collector came to report on his receipts. The figures in impressive columns covered page after page of parchment, and the collector's voice droned endlessly through a recital of the sums. But, in the end, Tamerlane was not satisfied. It seems that first this account and then that one had been misrepresented. In short, the tax collector had revealed himself as a scamp and a cheat.

"So *that* is the way you manage your post as tax collector!" raged the testy ruler. "Well, sir, I cannot swallow such outrageous lies. But"—and his eyes glinted—"*you* will swallow them. Begin at once!"

"Begin *what*, sire?" questioned the tax collector, puzzled and frightened.

"Begin to *swallow* your own accounts. Quickly, now. I have other business at hand." And the lordly Tamerlane watched with increasing amusement as the wretched collector choked and gagged on the sheets of parchment. At length he had chewed and swallowed them all, and his heroic effort was rewarded on the instant by Tameriane, who declared him no longer tax collector.

"Instead," declared Tamerlane, smiling broadly, "I appoint *you*, Nasreddin Hoca, to be my tax collector."

Appalled, the Hoca considered his sad plight. There was little doubt about the matter: no report could please Tamerlane. On the other hand, was it necessary to suffer such abuse for one's bookkeeping, however faulty? Suddenly the Hoca had a fine idea. This business might be managed, after all . . . Gravely he thanked Tamerlane for his fine evidence of trust in a simple hoca's judgment, and excused himself from the ruler's presence, to prepare himself for his new office.

Every morning during the following month, Nasreddin Hoca watched with tender concern as his wife rolled fine, fresh dough to paper thinness and baked it to form *yufka*, those platelike pastries. Then he took the pastries to one side and on them he recorded the tax receipts of the preceding day. With painstaking care he stacked the pastries in a special cupboard where they would be protected from prying eye and tampering touch.

Finally came the day of reckoning. Taking a large wheelbarrow loaded with the precious pastries, the Hoca trundled off to Tamerlane's court, and was admitted to the ruler's presence with his curious burden.

"Ah, there you are!" exclaimed Tamerlane, slapping his hands on his knees in great satisfaction. And, "Yes, yes," he murmured as he accepted the two large leather sacks containing the taxes collected. "But where are your accounts?"

"Right here, sire," replied the Hoca, gesturing toward the load in the wheelbarrow.

Tamerlane stared in disbelief. Then, "Bring me one of those things," he demanded.

Promptly the Hoca presented him with one of the pastries, covered from end to end with finely penned figures. As Tamerlane studied the inscriptions, a smile began to spread across his face. "And *what*, may I ask, was your purpose in keeping your records on pastry?"

"Only, sire, that *either one* of us might be able to swallow the reports of my labors," answered the Hoca.

The Hoca and the Candle

One day during a particularly bitter winter, the Hoca and his friends sat in the coffeehouse discussing the weather. Plain talk gave way to boasting, and before long the Hoca puffed out his chest importantly. "You may think we are having a cold winter. As for me, I thrive on cold and snow. Why, when I was a boy, I used to go out in the middle of January and break the ice on the river so that I could have a good, brisk swim for myself. Pooh! This cold is *nothing*."

This claim was too exaggerated for the rest of them. Nudging a companion, the Hoca's best friend set out a fine challenge. "I say, Hoca. You like cold weather. I suppose you could stay out all night long in the cold without a coat or a blanket and nothing at all to warm yourself?"

"Of course," bragged the Hoca.

"No fire, no hot tea, no blanket, no coat?" The others seemed impressed.

"Well," said the ringleader, "we'll make a bargain with you. If tonight you can stay outside, with absolutely nothing extra to warm you, all night long, you'll be our guest at a fine dinner. Right, friends?"

"Right!" they chorused.

"On the other hand," the ringleader continued, "if you use any means at all of keeping yourself warm, you will entertain us for dinner. How about that, Hoca effendi?"

"Fine, fine," agreed the Hoca.

That evening the Hoca's friends watched through the windows of their warm houses as the Hoca strolled here and there, studying the stars in the chill sky, and repenting a thousand times of his hasty, boastful tongue. Just as he was about to concede defeat, he spied a candle set in a window perhaps a hundred meters away. Fixing his eye on the candle glow, the Hoca felt the blood flow back through his stiffening veins. Thus he was able to endure the long night.

The next morning his friends, stepping outside into the frosty air, were amazed to find the Hoca calm and smiling, none the worse for his chill vigil. "Well, Hoca effendi, are you *sure* you used no means at all of warming yourself?" persisted the ringleader.

"No means at all," the Hoca declared, "unless you can call a candle a hundred meters away a means! I *did* see a candle burning, and its glow kept me equal to the torments of the cold."

"Aha!" exclaimed the challenger. "Hoca effendi, you must be our host at dinner, for you warmed yourself by that candle." No protest on the part of the Hoca was sufficient to move the resolve of his friends on the matter, so they were invited that evening to dinner at the Hoca's house.

The group arrived in good time, and sat on bolsters in the Hoca's sparsely furnished living room, waiting for the delicious smells that must herald a fine meal. But, sniff as they would, they could detect not a hint of what was to be served for dinner. What's more, the Hoca kept excusing himself to go out to the kitchen and supervise the cooking, a most unusual procedure for him. As one hour succeeded another with still no sign of food, the men began to grumble among themselves, and at last the ringleader chaffed the Hoca about the delay.

"Ah, my friends, you can come and see for yourselves that your dinner is being made ready," declared their host, and he led the way to the kitchen. Following him, they were amazed to find a large caldron suspended from the ceiling. A meter below the caldron burned a single candle.

"But, Hoca effendi," spluttered the ringleader, "surely you don't expect to heat that caldron with a *candle*? Why, the dinner would *never* get done!"

"Oh, I'm not so sure," answered the Hoca calmly. "If a candle a *hundred* meters away can keep me warm all night long, surely a candle one meter away can heat a caldron!"

Teeny-Tiny and
the Witch-Woman

Once there was and once there wasn't, long ago, when the flea was a porter and the camel a barber—well, in those times, there were three brothers, Big One, In-the-Middle, and Teeny-Tiny. Every morning their mother said, "Play here in the village, and I won't worry about you. But be sure not to go into the forest to play. Your granny says a witch-woman lives there and eats little children and uses their bones to make a fence around her house."

One day, though, not minding their mother at all, they went off to play in the forest. They wandered this way and that all day, and finally they could not find their way home. The shadows grew longer and longer, and night was near.

At last, Teeny-Tiny climbed a tree to look farther. "I see a light!" he called. They ran toward the light, and there was a little house, with a knobby little fence all around it. *Tok, tok, tok,* they knocked at the door, and an old woman hobbled to open it.

"Come in. Come in, my children," she cried, and in they went. Now, in truth, this woman was a witch, and she meant to eat them all. But first they must fall asleep, so she could tie their hands and feet and put them in her little cage.

She gave them a good hot supper and put them, one, two, three, to bed. She waited and waited, until after a while she did not hear a sound.

"Who is asleep and who is awake?" she called.

Now the others were asleep, but Teeny-Tiny was still awake, listening, and wondering about the knife the old woman was sharpening. "The littlest one is awake," he called at last.

"What, Teeny-Tiny! Why don't you sleep?" asked the old woman.

"Well, auntie, my mother always cooks me an egg before I go to bed. *Then* I go to sleep," said Teeny-Tiny.

So the old woman cooked an egg and Teeny-Tiny ate it. But still he did not go to sleep.

After a while, "Who is asleep and who is awake?" called the old woman.

And, "The littlest one is awake," answered Teeny-Tiny.

"What! Still awake? What will help you to go to sleep?" the woman asked.

"Well, auntie, my mother gives me popcorn and raisins to eat at bedtime. *Then* I go to sleep," said Teeny-Tiny.

So the old woman brought him popcorn and raisins, but still he did not go to sleep.

After a while, "Who is asleep and who is awake?" called the old woman.

And, "The littlest one is awake," answered Teeny-Tiny.

"What! Still awake, are you? What can I get you that will help you to sleep?" she asked.

"Well, auntie, that popcorn made me thirsty. At home, when I am thirsty, my mother goes to the well to fetch me water in a sieve. When she brings it back, I drink it, and *then* I sleep," said Teeny-Tiny.

The old woman took a sieve and started toward the well. As soon as she had stepped through the door, Teeny-Tiny shook his brothers. "Wake up!" he whispered. "Auntie is the witch our granny talked about. We must run away, or *we'll* be her dinner tomorrow!" And the boys hurried toward the door.

On a shelf by the door, Teeny-Tiny saw a round cake of soap, a needle, and a short sharp knife. "I may as well take these. Perhaps they will be useful," said he, and so he put them into his pocket. Away the three boys ran.

As for the old woman, she couldn't catch any water in the sieve and she *couldn't* catch any water in the sieve, so home she came. But when she looked for Teeny-Tiny, he was gone, and so, for that matter, were Big One and In-the-Middle. Away she went, running after them.

Now, Teeny-Tiny was watching behind him, and when he

could feel the old woman's breath on his neck, he turned and threw the cake of soap right at her. To his surprise, that round cake of soap grew and grew until it became a mountain, slippery all around. The boys kept on running, glad of that soap.

The old woman slipped and slithered and slid, trying to get up over that mountain, but it was no use. "I'll run *around* it," she decided, and she ran and ran till she came 'round to the other side. "*Now* I'll catch you!" she cried, and Teeny-Tiny heard her.

They kept running and running, till Teeny-Tiny could hear the old woman's apron flapping. Carefully he picked the needle out of his pocket and held it between his thumb and fingers. As soon as he felt the old woman's breath on his neck, he threw the needle at her. *Crick, snick!* That needle became a whole *mountain* of needles, all sticky and pricky and sharp as they could be.

Well, the boys ran on, glad of that needle. The old woman tried and tried to weave her way among the needles, but it was no use. She just couldn't climb that mountain. "I'll run *around* it," she decided, and she ran and ran till she came 'round to the other side. "*Now* I'll catch you!" she cried, and Teeny-Tiny heard her.

They kept running and running, till Teeny-Tiny heard her panting and puffing just behind them. Turning, he threw the knife just as hard as he could throw. That sharp knife cut a crack in the earth so long and so wide that the witch-woman couldn't run around it and she couldn't jump over it. Shaking her fist, she shouted, "I'll get you the *next* time!" And she turned around and hobbled home.

As for the three brothers, they never stopped running till they got to their own house. As for the witch-woman, may she wait a long, long time before she hears a knock at her door again.

Karaçor and the Giants

Once there was and twice there wasn't a poor man who had eleven sons. Time came, time went, and they became poorer and poorer. At last, the father said, "Sons, I can do no more for you. You must go forth to seek your own fortunes."

The ten older ones packed what few belongings they had, and set off down the road to the harbor. "Wait for me!" called Karaçor, the eleventh one. "I want to come, too."

"You are too young to come with us," the eldest said. "Stay and be a comfort to our old father." But Karaçor was determined to go, so, putting one foot after the other, and keeping well out of sight, he followed them.

The ten older ones at length boarded a ship. "Now at last we've left that nuisance of a Karaçor behind," said the eldest as they watched the shore fade from sight. "He would have been no use to us at all. Let him wander where he wishes!"

"And so I *did*," said Karaçor, and there he was, come aboard secretly after all. Since they couldn't very well throw him overboard, they agreed that he could come along with them.

For several days they sailed, until the ship came to another land. The eleven brothers took their belongings and went ashore. Perhaps in this place they would find their fortunes.

They walked and walked along the road that led from the harbor. "Aha!" said the eldest, pointing to a field of fine, ripe vegetables. "That would be a good place to fill our hungry stomachs."

"And that tree in the middle of the field would make a pleasant shade on this hot day," said the second son.

For his part, Karaçor was more curious than he was hungry, so while his older brothers were picking and eating tomatoes and carrots and cucumbers a-plenty, Karaçor climbed the tree to see what he could see. It was Karaçor who first saw the giant coming toward them with huge strides. Karaçor tucked himself in among the leafy branches to listen.

"Who told you that you could come into my field and eat? And why are you here, anyway?" roared the giant. "You've eaten my precious vegetables; now *I'll* eat *you*!"

"Oh, please don't!" begged the third of the ten older brothers. "We meant no harm. We are all brothers, and we were so hungry we never thought to ask whose field this was."

"We can work to pay for what we ate," said the eldest. "Try us!"

"Well," said the giant, "you *are* rather thin now for good eating. And you *might* be able to work hard enough to repay me for my vegetables. I'll make a bargain with you. There are ten of you, and only one of me. See that wheat field across the road? That belongs to me, too, and it's ripe for harvest. I'll reap the wheat in that field, and you will gather it into sheaves. If you can keep up with me, I'll let you go free. You will have earned what you ate. If you cannot do that, I'll fatten you well and eat you as payment for my good tomatoes and carrots and cucumbers."

The ten older brothers had no choice. "All right, sir. Start reaping!" And they worked—*how* they worked!—gathering into sheaves the wheat the giant reaped. But the giant with his huge sickle reaped half an acre with each slash of his sickle, and in a few minutes he was far ahead of the brothers. They had lost the bargain. So *this* was the fortune they had set forth to find . . .

As the giant was tucking the brothers under his arms to take them home for fattening, Karaçor called from the tree, "You may be going to eat *them*, but what are you going to do about *me*?"

Looking up, the giant saw Karaçor in the branches. "Oh, I'll eat you, too," he said, "but you're so small you'll hardly fill one of my back teeth."

"I'm small, it's true," said Karaçor, "but it's also true that I neither ate your precious vegetables nor made that bargain with you. I'll make a bargain of my own with you now. *I'll* reap, and *you* will sheave the stalks. If you can keep up with me, then you may fatten me and eat me, too. But if you cannot keep up with me, then my ten brothers and I shall eat *you*."

"You're a small one for that large bargain," said the giant as he set the older brothers down again. "I'll make short work of *this* bargain. Begin reaping!"

Karaçor took out his small sickle and began reaping little clumps of grain with it. But, guessing the giant's greediness, Karaçor scattered these clumps far and wide behind him, with every stalk in a different place and lying in a different direction. Since the giant did not want to lose a single grain of his harvest, he ran here, ran there, picking up one stalk at a time so that he could sheave all that was reaped. Bending, stooping, bending, stooping, he was soon overcome with heat and weariness. Finally the giant shouted, "Stop! Stop! You win!" Thus Karaçor saved not only himself but his ten older brothers, as well.

"Now," said the eldest brother, "*we* are going to eat *you*. And we'll not even need to fatten you to make a good meal for all of us!" And the ten older brothers took out their knives.

"Oh, *please* don't eat me!" begged the giant. "I have a wife and eleven daughters at home. What would they do without me? Why, right now, my wife is making the bread for our dinner. Come home with me and be our guests. I'll even give you my eleven daughters as your brides!"

While the ten brothers were talking this way and that about the matter, Karaçor ran on ahead to the giant's house. True enough, the giant's wife was kneading the dough for bread. And—as giantesses do—she had flung her huge breasts over her shoulders so they would not get in the way of her bread-making. Karaçor slipped up quietly behind her and began to suck at one of those huge breasts.

"Oh!" cried the giant's wife. "Who taught you to suck at the breast of a giantess? Now you are my milk child, and I cannot serve you to my giant husband for his dinner! But he will eat you if he finds you here, so I must protect you." Slap! She slapped Karaçor, turning him into a broom, and she put that broom behind the door.

Just then, the giant came into the yard with Karaçor's older brothers. "Wife, I smell a human being here," he roared.

"Nonsense, my husband," said his wife. "You must be smelling these ten young men you brought home for your dinner. There is no human being here besides these ten."

"Wife, there is a human being here. I can tell! Where? Where?" And he began to look around.

"Well, husband, you are right. A human being *did* come, but he sucked my breast and has become my milk child. If I bring him out, you must not hurt him. He is now like one of our own children," she said.

"That is true," the giant agreed. "Bring the milk child out. He is my son, too."

The giant mother brought out the broom, and Slap! There stood Karaçor.

"You!" exclaimed the giant. "Twice now you have tricked me today." Still, he kept his promise, and they all shared a good meal and a long evening's talk.

When bedtime came, all the sleeping mats for the giant's eleven daughters and for the eleven brothers were laid out in the same room, and all except Karaçor were soon sound asleep. As for Karaçor, he was curious: the giant and his wife kept whispering together, and they were sharpening and sharpening a great long knife. "I put kerchiefs on our daughters' heads and fezzes on the young men's heads, as you told me," the giant wife said.

"Good," said the giant. "As soon as this knife is well sharpened, I myself shall cut off all the heads that are wearing fezzes."

Well, Karaçor wasted no time: he quickly put the daughters' kerchiefs on his brothers' heads and on his own, and put the fezzes very nicely and firmly on the giants' daughters' heads. Then he slipped back into bed.

Feeling his way in the dark, the giant found the heads with fezzes, and, *slish, slish, slish,* one after another he cut the heads off. Then, satisfied with his night's work, he went to bed.

As soon as the giant had left, Karaçor awakened his brothers. "Get up! Get up!" he whispered. "We must get away from here! Follow me to the river at the end of the next field!"

His brothers groaned and grumbled, but they yanked the kerchiefs from their heads and followed Karaçor out of the window. Running, running, at last they reached the river and splashed across it to the other side. They were just in time, too, for there on the other side of the river was that giant, wanting to capture them but—as is true of giants—unable to cross the water.

"Come back!" the giant shouted. "I know what you did. You made me kill all eleven of my daughters!"

"We were guests in your house, and I am your milk son," called Karaçor. "The loss you had was your own doing. And now we'll be on our way."

The giant returned home, bitter but helpless. As for Karaçor and his brothers, they walked and walked until they came to the palace of a padişah, right in the center of a large town. *Tok, tok, tok!* They knocked at the door, and after a good bit of pleading, they were all given work to do at the palace.

Of all the eleven brothers, Karaçor soon became the padişah's favorite, and the older brothers grew jealous. "What can we do to get rid of this Karaçor?" they asked each other. "He has become almost a *son* of the padişah!" Finally they had agreed upon a plan that would surely cost Karaçor his life.

The eldest son gained permission to speak with the padişah. "My padişah," he said, "there is a giant who lives not many kilometers from here. That giant has a beautiful quilt just *covered* with pearls, a quilt suitable only for a great padişah like you."

"Aha! And how do you think I could get that quilt?"

"Our brother Karaçor could get it for you," the eldest said.

"Very well," said the padişah, and immediately he sent for Karaçor. After he had explained about the quilt, the padişah asked, "Can you get it for me?"

"Yes, my padişah, I can," said Karaçor.

"Will you need a large army?"

"No, my padişah. What I shall need are a box full of fleas and forty strips of cotton," answered Karaçor.

When he had received the box of fleas and the cotton strips, Karaçor set out in the dark for the giants' house. Once there, he tiptoed into the giants' bedroom and emptied the box of fleas over the bed. Thousands of fleas began to bite the giant and his wife. As the two itched and scratched and scratched and itched, their quilt slipped off the bed. Karaçor quickly stretched the strips of cotton between the rows of pearls so they would not click against each other. Then he folded up the quilt and ran away with it, holding it clear of the water as he splashed across the river.

By that time, the fleas had awakened the giants, and they reached for their quilt. It was gone! They searched inside the house; they searched outside the house. Just faintly in the distance they could see Karaçor, with something large in his arms. The giant went running, running, but of course he could not cross the river, so back he went to his own house.

As soon as the padişah awakened the next morning, Karaçor presented him with the quilt. The padişah was pleased, of course. But Karaçor's brothers, noticing the new favors heaped upon Karaçor, became more jealous than they had been before. "*Something* must be done to get rid of that Karaçor!" they grumbled. And finally they had agreed upon a plan that must surely succeed.

The eldest son again gained permission to speak with the padişah. "My padişah," he said, "that same giant has a very powerful and talented horse, a horse suitable only for a great padişah like you."

"Aha! And how do you think I could get that horse?"

"Our brother Karaçor could get it for you," the eldest said.

"Very well," said the padişah, and immediately he sent for Karaçor. After he had explained about the horse, the padişah asked, "Can you get it for me?"

"Yes, my padişah, I can," said Karaçor.

"Shall I summon my cavalry?"

"No, my padişah. What I shall need are a bag of mixed peanuts and hazelnuts, a silver saddle, and a long roll of felt."

When he had received the bag of nuts, the silver saddle, and the roll of felt, Karaçor set out in the evening dusk for the giant's house. Once there, he went quietly, quietly, into the stable. He whispered to the horse, "I have brought you a whole bag of peanuts and hazelnuts. If I put all these in your nosebag, will you come along with me for a little ride?"

"Of course I will," said the horse softly, "as long as you give me the whole bagful at once."

"I shall," said Karaçor. "And I have a silver saddle for your

back. I brought also a roll of felt to stretch before you so that
your hoofs will be as quiet as this dark night. I'll ride you for
just a little while."

"All right," agreed the horse.

At once, Karaçor saddled the horse. Quickly he unrolled the
felt to make a soundless pathway. Then he placed the nut-filled
nosebag on the horse so he could munch at will.

"*Deh!*" whispered Karaçor, and the horse began to step with
all his power. Away they went!

As the two left the stable, some small noise startled the
giant, and he awoke. "Woman!" he shouted. "There's a noise
in our stable. Wake up! Can someone be stealing our horse?"

"Only that Karaçor would dare . . ." the giant wife began.

"Karaçor! It's that Karaçor!" raged the giant. "I'll catch him
this time and make him pay for his tricks!"

But no matter how fast the giant ran, Karaçor and the horse
kept ahead of him. They forded the river, leaving the giant on
the other side, beating his knees in grief. As for the wife, she
had panted along behind him, and she, too, beat her knees in
grief. "Oh, that Karaçor!" she moaned. "He has cost us our
daughters and our quilt, and now our horse . . . lost! lost! They
are all lost!"

In a little while, Karaçor arrived at the padişah's stables,
where he left the horse to be cared for. Carrying the silver saddle,
he returned it to the padişah.

Of all the padişah's subjects, Karaçor's brothers were most
amazed at this remarkable feat—amazed, and jealous beyond
measure. "This time he must be given a task from which he
cannot return," said the eldest one, and the other nine brothers
agreed. By talking this way and that, they finally had a plan that
would finish their troublesome youngest brother forever.

Once more, the eldest son gained permission to speak with
the padişah. "My padişah," he said, "have you ever seen a
giant?"

"No," answered the padişah, "but I have always wanted to
see one. Do you suppose that Karaçor could bring that giant
here to my palace?"

"If *anyone* could, our Karaçor could," said the brother. "Shall
I carry the news to Karaçor?"

"By no means," said the padişah. "I want to tell him myself. Tell him only that I want to see him."

The eldest brother hurried to summon Karaçor to the padişah's presence. Then he shared the news with his jealous brothers.

As soon as the padişah had returned Karaçor's greeting, he said, "My son, I have one more thing to ask of you. I want to see this giant of yours. Can you bring him here?"

"Most certainly, my padişah," said Karaçor.

"Let's see . . . you will need both my army and my cavalry . . ."

"Indeed not, my padişah. All I shall need are some ragged clothes to fit me, a large gray moustache, a long gray beard, and an axe—a *blunt* axe," said Karaçor. Surprised, the padişah ordered exactly what was needed.

As soon as these things were provided, Karaçor dressed himself in the ragged clothes, glued the moustache and the beard to his face, and put the blunt axe over his shoulder. He looked the very picture of an old, old woodcutter.

Just after midday, he crossed the river, entered the giant's walnut grove, and began to chop at a tree, all the while chanting a tuneless song: "*Chut*! That Karaçor at last is dead! *Chut*! And I've been sent to make his coffin! *Chut*!"

The giant, hearing the distant sound of chopping, rushed from his dinner straight to the walnut grove. "What are you doing to my precious tree, you stupid old man? And what is it that you keep singing as you work?"

"Oh, that?" asked Karaçor. "That evil Karaçor kept doing this and that bad thing, and finally the padişah caught him and killed him. Now *I've* been sent with this axe to make a walnut coffin for the rascal. It's a long, hard job for an old man, but all of us are glad to know he's dead. *Chut*! That Karaçor at last is dead! *Chut*! And I've been sent to make his coffin! *Chut*!" And with each *Chut*! the old woodcutter took another chip out of the giant's walnut tree.

"What a blunt axe you have!" exclaimed the giant. "Karaçor is dead! Karaçor is dead!" he chanted as he hurried home for his large, sharp axe. *Tak-tuk-tak-tuk*! The giant chopped with mighty strokes, and because he was so glad of that trickster

Karaçor's death, the giant had finished a large, sturdy coffin for Karaçor in just a little over an hour.

"I *do* hope it will fit him!" said the woodcutter, studying the length and breadth of the coffin. "I've seen him only once, so I can't be sure the coffin's big enough."

"Still, he must be smaller than I am, so if the coffin is big enough for me, it should be big enough for him," said the giant. "Here. Let me get inside so you can measure."

"What a good idea," said the woodcutter. "You've done all of the hard work. Now just lie still and rest for a little bit while I see whether the lid will close over that Karaçor!" And *tunk-tunk-tunk-tunk*, he hammered in nail after nail. "How does it fit?" he called. "Does it pinch anywhere?" And all the time, he was hammering in more nails.

Then he tied a very strong rope around and around the coffin, a rope that the giant himself had brought to haul the coffin with.

"What are you doing?" asked the giant. "Haven't you finished measuring yet? It's getting very hot and stuffy in here!"

"Uh-huh. Just let me finish what I'm doing, and we'll be all ready." And he pulled with all his strength to get the coffin across the river.

"Hey, you stupid old man!" shouted the giant. "I can hear water outside. This has gone far enough! Where are you taking me? And who *are* you, anyway?"

"Where? Why, to the padişah, of course. He said he wanted to see a giant, and the only one willing to take you there was that rascal Karaçor. And who am I? I am Karaçor!" And he kept dragging the coffin and dragging the coffin, tug by tug by tug, until at last he reached the padişah's palace. As for the giant, he kept crying to get out and crying to get out, and beating and beating on the coffin lid that he himself had made for Karaçor.

By the time they reached the palace, a great crowd of people had gathered, and "Karaçor has brought the giant! Karaçor has brought the giant!" they chanted. Then, "Open it up! Let us see the giant!" they shouted until their throats were hoarse.

"It is not for me to open it," said Karaçor. "It was *my* task to bring the giant here. My ten brothers will open the coffin after I have left." When the padişah heard Karaçor say that he was leaving, he said, "You have served me well indeed. Now, ask whatever you wish, and it will be granted."

"My padişah," said Karaçor, "I ask only the giant's horse, the silver saddle, and a saddlebag with money in it to buy my bread and cheese."

"You may have all of those things," said the padişah, and he ordered that the pockets of the saddlebag be filled with gold. Well satisfied, Karaçor saddled and mounted the horse and galloped away, *chick-a-dock, chick-a-dock, chick-a-dock.*

It was time now for the crowd to see the giant. The padişah, befitting his rank, stood at the head of the coffin, eager to have the first look at this remarkable creature. The ten older brothers shivered and shook as they started to loosen the lid of the coffin. When they had taken out only half of the nails, the giant put his full strength against the lid and burst out of the coffin, breaking the padişah's skull with the edge of the lid. In his rage, the giant strangled, one after another, all ten of Karaçor's brothers. Then, his anger cooled, he left, glad to be free of that coffin.

And Karaçor? He went home to find his father.

"Greetings, my son. But where are your brothers?" his father asked. "There were eleven of you when you left. Did they make their fortunes?"

"Father, they made the fortunes they deserved. Ten of them were not worthy to be called your sons, and they have had the reward they earned. But let us now begin to live a rich and comfortable life together." And so they did.

Three apples fell from the sky, one for the teller of this tale, one for the listener, and the third for the one who asks "Where is mine? Where is *mine?*"

The Wonderful Pumpkin

Once there was and twice there wasn't, when jinns played polo in the old Turkish bath, when the flea was a porter and the camel a barber—well, in those times there was a poor widow who had one son. Hour after hour, day after day, the old woman sat making fine lace. Each market day, her son took the lace to a corner of the bazaar and sold it for what few kuruş he could get. With these coins he bought bread and cheese and olives, and somehow with Allah's help they managed to keep skin and bones together.

One day, however, the boy was unable to sell a single length of lace. Tired and disheartened, he sat on a stone and moaned to himself, "*Oof*, what shall I do? *Oof, oof!*"

At that moment, the *oof* jinn appeared, with one lip in the sky and the other touching the ground. "Ask what you wish, and it will be granted," said the jinn.

The boy was so startled that his tongue stuck to the roof of his mouth. At last he stammered, "I wish only your good health, sire."

"Ask what you wish, and it will be granted," the jinn repeated.

And, "I wish only your good health, sire," the boy answered, his eyes staring half out of his head.

"Ask what you wish, and it will be granted," the jinn said, and the ground trembled with the rumble of his voice.

Finally the boy found courage to speak. "Today I could not sell the lace my mother made. She will be angry with me. And we have nothing at all in the house to eat."

"Here. Take this," replied the jinn, handing the boy a small pumpkin.

"Thank you," the boy said, "but a pumpkin is of no use to us. We have neither charcoal to cook it nor sugar to sweeten it."

"You need neither charcoal nor sugar for *this* pumpkin. Merely say, 'Open, tiny little squash. Shut, tiny little pumpkin.'" And the jinn disappeared.

Puzzled, the boy stared about him. Then, clutching the pumpkin, he ran home.

His mother, watching for him in the doorway, was disgusted when she saw what he had. "My boy," she cried, "what am I to do with a *pumpkin*? I trusted you with the lace, and see what a fool you have made of yourself with our money!"

Quietly the boy put the pumpkin on the table. "Open, tiny little squash," said he. And immediately all sorts of good foods came pouring from the pumpkin. With rice and meats and beans and sweets before her, how could any woman quarrel about the pumpkin? The two sat down and ate happily until their stomachs were filled.

They were so happy that they did not see their greedy neighbor Mehmet passing by the window. Mehmet stopped to stare astonished at what he saw inside. He could almost taste each delicious dish as he stood and watched. At last, when the boy and his mother had finished eating, the boy said, "Shut, tiny little pumpkin." In a blink, the rest of the food disappeared, and the pumpkin sat on the table just like any other pumpkin.

The boy put the wonderful pumpkin in front of the window, and at length he and his mother went to bed. As soon as they had fallen asleep, Mehmet reached in through the window and grasped the pumpkin. Eagerly he hurried home with it.

All night long, Mehmet tried to open the pumpkin. "Open, pumpkin. *Open*, pumpkin!" he cried. But the pumpkin would not open. "Open, gourd. Open!" he said. But the pumpkin would not open. Mehmet knocked the pumpkin on the floor, on the table, on the chair, but it *still* would not open. He cut away at it with a knife, but not a mark was left on the pumpkin shell. By morning, he was thoroughly disgusted. "I shall *sell* it," he decided, "since I cannot open it. But I shall sell it for a great deal of money, since it is a very valuable pumpkin."

That morning, Mehmet tucked the pumpkin under his arm and went straight to the grocer. "You *sell* all day long," Mehmet said, "but I have something you will want to *buy*."

"A pumpkin? Why should I want a pumpkin?"

"Ah, but this is no ordinary pumpkin," Mehmet replied. "If you know how to open it, it will feed you all your life."

"How do you open it?" asked the grocer curiously.

"I wish I knew," answered Mehmet. "If I knew, I would keep it myself. Just think! I am willing to sell this wonderful pumpkin to you for only three gold liras."

"Three gold liras!" the grocer exclaimed. "And you cannot even tell me how to open it? Get along with your pumpkin! Perhaps you will find some fool to give you what you ask, but it won't be Hamit the grocer. Three gold liras, indeed!"

Mehmet snuggled the pumpkin under his arm and hurried down the street to the butcher's. "You sell good meat," Mehmet said, "but I have something better for you. Will you buy it?"

The butcher stared at Mehmet. "A pumpkin? What makes you think I want a pumpkin?"

"But," Mehmet said, "this is not just an *ordinary* pumpkin. If you know how to open it, it will feed you all your life."

"How *do* you open it?" asked the butcher.

"Ah, I wish I knew," sighed Mehmet. "If I knew, I would keep it myself. I will sell this wonderful pumpkin to you for only three gold liras."

"Three gold liras!" gasped the butcher. "You may keep it yourself, for all of me. If I cannot open it, I cannot use it. Get you gone with your pumpkin, now. Out, out!"

Hastily, Mehmet left the butcher shop. Still holding the pumpkin, he entered the barbershop. "Oh, barber, you listen all day to the troubles of the poor, and your heart is moved to help them. This time, I have come to do *you* a favor. I have a wonderful pumpkin to sell you."

"It looks like any ordinary pumpkin to me. What is so wonderful about it?" asked the barber.

"If you know how to open it, it will feed you all your life."

"And how do you open it?" The barber stared curiously at the pumpkin.

"I wish I knew," Mehmet answered sadly. "If I knew how

to open it, I would keep it myself. Surely *you* can open it. I shall sell it to you for only three gold liras."

"Three gold liras!" the barber shouted. "What kind of fool do you think I am? Get out, before I shave your ears off and leave you looking like a pumpkin yourself!"

Mehmet scurried out of the barbershop. *Now* where could he go? "Ah, the judge will see the worth of this pumpkin," muttered Mehmet, and he carried the pumpkin to the judge's house. "Sire," said Mehmet, "you know a good case from a bad one. I have a fine pumpkin here, just for you. Will you buy it?"

The judge looked thoughtfully at the pumpkin. "How much are you asking for it?"

"Very *little* for such a wonderful pumpkin," Mehmet replied. "If you know how to open it, this pumpkin will feed you all your life. That is why I am asking three gold liras for it."

"How do you open it?"

"Alas, I do not know how to open it," Mehmet said. "If I knew how to open it, you may be sure I would keep it myself!"

The judge knew greedy Mehmet very well. "Mehmet, if *you* cannot open it, *I* cannot," said the judge. "I will buy it just as any ordinary pumpkin. And, since you are one of Allah's poor souls, I shall even give you a whole gold lira for it, but not *three* gold liras. No, indeed."

Sighing, Mehmet accepted the gold lira, and after he had left, the judge took the pumpkin to his wife. "Here, my dear," he said. "We shall have fresh pumpkin for dinner."

A few moments later, his wife came back carrying the pumpkin. "How am I to cook this pumpkin if I cannot even open it?" she asked. "I can't cut it with a knife; I can't break it with an axe."

"That Mehmet!" exclaimed the judge. "I should have known better than to buy anything from him. Here, my dear, give me the pumpkin. It is fit for nothing but the trash heap. Tomorrow, find yourself a fine, fresh pumpkin at the market." And the judge threw the pumpkin away.

Meanwhile, the boy and his mother had looked in vain all day for their pumpkin. Finally, the boy chanced to pass the judge's house on his way home from evening prayers at the mosque. There on a heap of rubbish lay a small pumpkin. Could it be *his* pumpkin? Almost without hope, the boy said, "Open, tiny little squash." Immediately, all sorts of good foods began to pour from the pumpkin. Overjoyed, the boy ran to the rubbish heap. "Shut, tiny little pumpkin," he ordered, and the foods disappeared. Picking up the pumpkin, the boy ran all the way home with it. As soon as he was inside, he closed the door and covered the window. "Come, Mother," he called. "I have found our pumpkin. Let us eat."

From that time on, the boy kept the pumpkin safely hidden, and he and his mother lived comfortably together. They had their wish fulfilled; may we be as lucky in ours.

The Courage of Kazan

Once there was and once there wasn't, when the flea was a porter and the camel a barber—well, in those times there was a timid fellow named Kazan. Since Kazan's father was dead, Kazan and his mother took turn and turn about guarding the sheep that belonged to the families in their village. In exchange, they received enough bread and cheese to keep skin and bones together.

It chanced one day that Kazan was watching the sheep in the field when he noticed a gray shadow slipping along at the edge of the pasture. Of a sudden, he thought, "What if that should be a wolf? How could I save these sheep, or even myself, without help?" All a-tremble, he ran straight home. "Mother, I cannot guard the sheep another day," he said. "I have not enough courage to be out there alone with wolves in the shadows."

His mother talked this way and that, but Kazan's mind was set upon the matter. As for his mother, she was every bit as sure that if Kazan would not work, Kazan should not eat. From that time forth, Kazan stayed at home, and he was given not so much as a crust of bread or a rind of cheese until he should come to his senses and go back to work with the sheep.

But, alas, habit is in truth worse than rabies. The more Kazan thought about wolves, the less ready he felt to go forth into the pasture, and finally he said as much to his mother.

"Ah, my boy," she sighed, "what good are you this way either to yourself or to me? Here, take the bit of money your father left for you, and go out into the world to find your courage. You are less than half a man without it."

After kissing his mother's hands, Kazan set out, putting one foot before the other on the long road that lay ahead of him. Where, then, did one go to look for courage?

In the next village, Kazan bought a loaf of bread and a small packet of *helva,* and he sat just beyond the town in the shade of a gnarled old olive tree to eat his lunch. Feeling tired from his long walk, he closed his eyes for a moment to rest, and in three or five breaths he was sound asleep.

While he slept, great swarms of flies began to gather about the crumbs of helva on his knees, and with a bizzing and a buzzing they dined at his expense. Kazan, who was dreaming all the while of wolves and such creatures, suddenly brought his hands down with a sound WHACK on both knees, and in the whacking he woke himself up. To his surprise, he found forty flies dead on his lap.

"What is this!" he exclaimed. "I have been walking just a short while, and I have already begun to find my courage. All my life I have been afraid of flies, and here I have been brave enough to kill forty at one stroke. I must tell the world about it."

Rising immediately, he hurried into the town. There he found a blacksmith and bought from him a huge sword. On its handle he had the following words made plain for all to see: "Kazan, killer of forty souls at one stroke." Giving the blacksmith the last of his money, Kazan picked up the sword and carried it proudly along the road. "Now," said he, "I shall test to see if I have really found my courage."

He walked along and walked along, meeting no one in his walking, until at last he came to a public fountain. *Luk-luk-luk,* he drank, for he was very thirsty. "I shall sit here for just a minute to rest, and then I shall go on," he decided. But in truth the poor fellow was more tired than he knew, for no sooner had he sat down than his head drooped forward on his breast and he was sound asleep, with his gleaming new sword close beside him.

While he was sleeping, a troop of the sultan's soldiers came *chick-a-dock, chick-a-dock, chick-a-dock,* all in a gallop down the road. They stopped at the fountain to water their horses, and while they idled there, the captain chanced to notice Kazan's sword. Bending closer to read what was written on the handle, he shouted, "What is this! These days, courage comes in strange packages, indeed. This fellow claims he has killed forty souls at a single stroke."

"Aha!" exclaimed another. "Then he is just the man to kill the monster." And the others readily agreed.

Their loud talk awakened Kazan, who went weak as water at the sight of the soldiers' bold moustachios and flashing eyes. He reached for his sword, but his hands shook so that he could scarcely lift it. "Ah, me," he thought. "I have not found my courage, after all. I was mistaken."

The soldiers looked anxiously at one another. This hero was clearly all of a tremble with rage at being awakened. It would be wise to tread carefully in dealing with him.

"Please, sire, do not draw your sword," urged the captain. "We have great need of a man with your courage. Surely a man who has killed forty souls with a single stroke can kill the monster which is ravaging our country."

"Monster!" thought Kazan. And he cast about in his mind for a way to tell these soldiers that the forty he had slain were merely flies.

But, "Come with me," said the captain. "Our sultan will make you welcome in his palace. He will tell you about the monster." And he made room on his own horse for Kazan.

For his part, Kazan had no wish to ride a horse. To tell the truth, he feared horses even more than he feared flies. "Not I!" he said firmly. Then, ashamed to tell the soldiers he was afraid of horses, he added, "There is no horse living which is equal to my needs. Until I find such a horse, I shall walk." And he set off at a brisk pace down the road.

In a short time, Kazan and the soldiers arrived before the sultan. "Here, your majesty, is a true hero. He will rid your kingdom of the monster," the captain said.

The sultan stared at Kazan. "What makes you so sure you can kill the monster?" he asked. "That dreadful creature has destroyed all my finest soldiers. To keep him from attacking the palace, I have been forced to give him three men a week for his food. Where did you ever find such courage?"

But before Kazan could say that, indeed, he had no courage

at all, the captain of the guards spoke for him. "Sire, on the handle of his sword are these words: 'Kazan, killer of forty souls at a single stroke.' Surely such a brave man can kill the monster."

Suddenly the sultan smiled. "You, Kazan with the sword, I like your modesty. No brave man needs to say that he has courage. He shows his courage on the field of battle. Go now with my vizier. He will take you to the most elegant chamber in my palace. Tomorrow when the monster comes, you will ride forth to meet him."

Kazan, still unable to confess that he was a coward, not a hero, turned to follow the vizier. But all the while, the word "monster" was churning in his head. How he wished that he had found his courage! But he had no courage at all, poor fellow—not a single pocketful. Something must be done, and that right quickly, or he would have an adventure quite apart from his own choosing.

After the vizier had left him in his fine chamber, timid Kazan went to the window to see what he could see. To the east of the village stretched vast brown plains. "No hiding place for me there," sighed Kazan. To the west of the village lay more brown plains. "No escape for me that way," groaned Kazan. Then he looked to the north. There lay woods and forests as far as the eye could see.

"With Allah's help," decided Kazan, "I shall make my way through the trees. I cannot meet that monster in the morning. I have not even courage enough to tweak his ear, to say nothing of taking his life." So saying, he awaited the coming of dark, when he could make his escape.

As soon as the last bit of light had faded from the sky, Kazan opened his door a tiny crack and looked outside. Soldiers stood guard at both ends of the long corridor. To go that way was clearly impossible. Quietly, Kazan closed the door again, and, picking up his sword, he went to the window. With one stroke of the blade, he shattered the glass. Then he leaped from the window, landing by pure good fortune on a great heap of hay. "Allah finds a low branch for the bird that cannot fly," he murmured, and, painfully picking himself up, he limped away toward the north.

For the first hour or so, he put one foot before the other as fast as ever he could, until he had reached the shelter of the trees. Suddenly, as a twig snapped beneath his feet, he remembered the monster. His heart began to pound within his breast. Suppose the monster should be hiding among the trees? Flinging his sword to one side, Kazan scrambled up the nearest tree, and hid trembling in its branches.

By winding his legs around the nearest large branch, Kazan was able to keep himself from falling. But for most of the long night, cold fear kept him awake. Who knew when the monster might appear?

His eyelids heavy from weariness, poor Kazan had at last barely begun to nod off to sleep when he felt the whole tree shake. Looking directly beneath him, Kazan saw in the misty morning light the most horrible monster that had ever been let loose in the world. Kazan's knees turned to water. His tongue clove to the roof of his mouth. His hands began to shake. "How could I ever have thought I was afraid before?" he murmured. "Now I have real need of courage, and I have none—none at all!" He groaned, his teeth chattering all the while.

The monster, who had seen Kazan in the branches, continued to butt his huge head against the tree trunk until at last he shook Kazan right out of the tree. As Allah would have it, timid Kazan found himself sitting squarely on the monster's back. Clutching the creature's ears, Kazan held tightly as the beast shook and turned and leaped in an effort to throw Kazan off his back. Somehow, Kazan stuck fast as a thorn, and at last the monster stopped leaping and began to run straight toward the sultan's palace.

Meanwhile, the vizier had gone to summon Kazan and had found his room empty. Seeing the window broken, he exclaimed, "Now I understand! The brave fellow was not willing to wait for the monster, but has gone forth to seek him out." And he hurried to give the sultan the good news.

Just as the vizier had entered the sultan's chamber, there arose a great outcry beneath the window. Running to the window, the sultan and the vizier beheld surely the strangest sight that had ever been seen in the kingdom. With Kazan firmly seated on the creature's back and clutching both his ears, there came the monster, rushing toward the palace at full speed. And on one hand and another, all the brave soldiers of the sultan's guard ran to meet him, each wanting to be the first to strike the monster.

As it happened, the captain gained the first stroke, with the others striking immediately after. Kazan had such a tight grip of the ears that the captain had to cut off the ears one at a time to release the hero from his seat. "So this is the kind of steed that is worthy of you!" exclaimed the captain as he helped the weary victor to the ground. Kazan kept his own counsel, but he was happy indeed to feel the earth firm beneath his feet.

"Oh, my brave warrior!" said the sultan. "Who but a true hero would have been bold enough to bring home a monster by the ears? There is but one thing more that I will ask of you. I want you to be the man to lead my troops against the sultan of the next kingdom. For far too long, he has threatened my borders, and I have at last declared war upon him. With your help, we are certain to win."

Delighted with the brave Kazan, the sultan ordered ten of his servants to carry the hero in a litter to the place of honor in his banquet hall. There, Kazan was fed upon the finest foods in the kingdom, with a special drink of birds' milk into the bargain.

The morning of the battle dawned only too soon, and Kazan was summoned to appear before the sultan. "You are such a bold and brave man," said the sultan, "that I have decided to send you out alone as our champion against the enemy forces. Go now to the stable and select a noble steed."

Kazan, with his heart in his throat, went anon to the stable, holding well to the wall to avoid the stamping hoofs and gleaming teeth of the sultan's war-horses. Looking from one to another, he said at last to the groom, "I see no horse here that I can ride into battle."

"What!" The groom was astonished. "These are the finest horses to be found in forty kingdoms."

"That may be," retorted Kazan, "but not a one of them suits me."

Suddenly as he looked in the farthest corner of the stable he spied a swaybacked steed with broken teeth and glazed eyes. Of *that* horse he need not be afraid, he thought. "Well, after all,

I have found my horse," he said, pointing to the steed in the corner.

Scratching his head in disbelief, the groom led forth the stumbling creature. "Look!" he exclaimed. "This poor thing can scarcely stand. How do you expect to ride him forth to battle?"

"Only keep him on his feet while I mount," said Kazan, "and you will see. He and I will suit each other far better than you dream."

Now, in truth, though Kazan did not know it, the old steed was a fine battle horse, the sire of all the other steeds in the stable, and he quivered with excitement as he was led forth into the sunshine. "Here," said Kazan to the groom, handing him a rope fifty meters long. "I shall lie down on the horse. You must bind me to his back with this rope."

Shaking his head doubtfully, the groom wound the rope around and around the young champion until he could move not a single hair. "Now, let him go forth," said Kazan, and the old horse ran full tilt into what was after all the business he knew best. And Kazan, half paralyzed by fright, had no choice but to go along into battle himself.

One after another, the old war-horse sought out the enemy, biting anyone who came toward him from the front and kicking anyone who approached him from the rear. In the confusion of the battle, three or five meters of the rope binding Kazan came unwound and trailed along the ground. As it dragged, it caught in the trunk of a fallen pine tree with many branches, and the pine tree came along behind, knocking many of the enemy horsemen from their mounts. The enemy was routed so badly by this strange new weapon that in no time at all a messenger came bearing the flag of truce.

The war-horse, not knowing the language of flags, continued to bite and kick until the whole enemy army was destroyed. Only those who fled the battlefield escaped with their lives. Finally, the horse returned to the sultan's stable with Kazan still bound to his back. As the groom unbound him and helped him to the ground, Kazan said, feeling rather more cheerful now that the battle was over, "Well, we have not only defeated the enemy but we have also brought you enough firewood for three or five years."

During the next few months, the whole kingdom was a-buzz with talk of Kazan's courage. For his part, Kazan said to himself, "As far as I can see, I still have no courage at all. But fortunately, a man is judged by his work. If others wish to call me brave, that's well and good with me. Perhaps by looking brave, I may one day in truth find courage. Meanwhile, whatever I have instead of it must see me through."

In time, Kazan married the sultan's beautiful daughter, in a wedding that lasted forty days and forty nights, and all their wishes were fulfilled. May we have a bit of their good fortune.

Riddles

I looked in the evening and there were many;
I got up in the morning and there were not any.
(Stars)

It has a city, but houses it has not;
It has a railroad, but trains it has not;
It has a lake, but water it has not.
Now guess what this is!
(Map)

Looks like sugar; sweet is not;
Flies in the air; no wings has got.
(Snow)

Just Say *Hiç*!

Once there was and twice there wasn't, when God's creatures were many and it was a sin to talk too much—well, in those times there was a man who had a simpleminded servant boy named Hasan.

This Hasan was a good enough servant except for one thing: he never could remember from one minute to the next what he was told to do.

"Hasan!" called his master one day. "Here is a penny. Take it to the market and buy some salt."

Hasan took the penny and put it into the pocket of his baggy trousers. "Salt," he thought. "How can I remember salt?" This time he was determined to remember what he was told. "I know," he decided at last. "I'll say it over and over and over, all the way to the market. That way, I'll be sure to remember what I'm supposed to say."

In Hasan's village, the common word for salt was *hiç*. So "*Hiç, hiç, hiç,*" Hasan said to himself, as he scuff-scuffed in his flat shoes along the dusty road to the market.

And "*Hiç, hiç, hiç,*" he said, as he stopped to watch a peasant fishing in a little stream under the bridge.

Hasan was determined not to forget what he had been told to say, but he did like to watch people fishing. So "*Hiç, hiç, hiç,*" he kept saying as he watched.

Now, in most parts of Turkey, the word *hiç* means "nothing," and nothing is exactly what the fisherman caught while Hasan stood there saying "*Hiç!*"

Finally the fisherman became very angry. "You're not supposed to say that!" he shouted.

Hasan was quite surprised. "What am I supposed to say, then?" he asked.

And the fisherman answered, "You should say, 'May there be three or five of them! May there be three or five of them!' That's what you should say."

Hasan was so eager to remember what he was told that he began to repeat, "May there be three or five of them! May there be three or five of them!" When he was quite sure he would remember it, he went scuff-scuffing in his flat shoes along the dusty road toward the market.

On the road he met a funeral procession. As he watched the procession moving along, he chanted to himself, "May there be three or five of them! May there be three or five of them!"

A man in the crowd heard Hasan and became very angry. "Boy," he said, "you're not supposed to say that!"

Hasan was puzzled. "Then what *am* I supposed to say?" he asked.

The man said, "You should say, 'May Allah bless his soul! May Allah bless his soul!' That's what you should say."

Hasan repeated after him, "May Allah bless his soul! May Allah bless his soul!" When he was sure he could remember what he was supposed to say, he walked on toward the market.

As he went along, murmuring, "May Allah bless his soul!" he sniffed something strange. Following his nose, he came to a dead dog at the edge of the road. "May Allah bless his soul! May Allah bless his soul!" he muttered, as he looked down at the dead dog.

Just then a man came along and heard Hasan talking. When he came near and looked down, he saw nothing but a dead dog.

"Boy, are you crazy?" he exclaimed. "You're not supposed to say that!"

Hasan was more puzzled than before. "What am I supposed to say, then?" he asked.

The man told him, "You should say, 'Ugh! What a smell! Ugh! What a terrible smell!' That's what you should say."

Hasan's nose told him that this was indeed true. In order to be sure to remember what he should say, he began repeating over and over, "Ugh! What a smell! Ugh! What a terrible smell!"

On he went, saying it over and over, so he would not forget what he had been told.

As Hasan walked along, three ladies came out of a Turkish bath, all three as clean and shiny as could be. They heard Hasan say, "Ugh! What a smell! Ugh! What a terrible smell!"

Well, the ladies laid down their bath dippers and threw stones at him, shouting, "How can you say that? How *dare* you say that?"

Poor Hasan was really confused. "Then, what *am* I supposed to say!" he asked the ladies.

And one of them answered, "You should say, 'My, how nice! Oh, how nice!' That's what you should say."

"Yes," the other ladies agreed. "You should say, 'My, how nice! Oh, how nice!'"

Hasan bowed, and he began to say, "My, how nice! Oh, how nice!"

The three ladies nodded and smiled as Hasan went scuff-scuffing down the road toward the market, saying just what he was supposed to say.

He was still saying, "My, how nice! Oh, how nice!" when he came to two men fighting. He stood there awhile and watched the fight, saying, "My, how nice!" as the first man hit the second man, and "Oh, how nice!" as the second man hit the first man.

Well, the two men became so angry when they heard what he said that they stopped fighting each other, and each of them gave Hasan a good stout blow for his trouble. "You're not supposed to say that!" the first man said, as he gave the boy another blow for good measure.

Bewildered, Hasan asked, "What am I supposed to say, then?"

The second man answered, "You should say, 'Don't do that, gentlemen! Don't fight, please!'"

"Yes, that's what you should say," said the first man.

As Hasan went on down the road, he repeated, "Don't do that, gentlemen! Don't fight, please!" until he was sure he could remember what he was supposed to say.

Just down the street from the market, he saw two dogs fighting. "Don't do that, gentlemen! Don't fight, please!" he kept saying, greatly interested all the time in watching the fight.

A man standing near him said, "Are you crazy? You're not supposed to say that!"

Hasan's eyes opened wide in surprise. "Then, what am I supposed to say?"

"Well," the man said, "you just say, 'Get out, dog! Go away, dog!' That's what you should say."

Hasan continued on his way. "Get out, dog! Go away, dog!" he chanted over and over as he entered the market.

At the first shop in the marketplace, the shoemaker sat working on a shoe. He was holding a piece of leather in his mouth and stretching it out big enough to make a pair of shoes. When he heard Hasan saying as he passed, "Get out, dog! Go away, dog!" the shoemaker spat out the leather angrily and shouted, "The dog is yourself! You're not supposed to say that!"

By this time, Hasan was completely befuddled. "Please don't be angry with me," he said. "Tell me. What *am* I supposed to say?"

And the shoemaker said, "Boy, you should say nothing! Just say *hiç!*"

"Oh, thank you!" cried Hasan happily. "*That's* what I was supposed to remember!"

And he went a little farther on and bought the salt.

How Deli Kept His
Part of the Bargain

Once there was and twice there wasn't, when yesterday was today and the sieve lay in the hay—well, in those days there were three friends, Ahmet, Mehmet, and *Deli*. Hard times had fallen upon the country, and, try as they would, the three friends could find no work to do for their daily bread and cheese, until at last each of the three had but one gold lira left in his shabby pocket. They met one morning by the village fountain to find some means out of their misery.

"I have tried to find work on every plot of ground from here to the next village," said Ahmet, "and there is no work to be had."

"For my part," said Mehmet, "I have asked at every shop both here and in the next village that I might become an apprentice, and none would give me a place."

"And I," said Deli, "have gone from coffeehouse to coffeehouse begging work, and I have gained nothing but scowls for my pains."

"See here," said Ahmet. "This sad state of affairs cannot last forever. If we could just manage to live from hand to mouth for two or three more months, harvest time would be at hand, and we could perhaps find work here and there in the fields. I have a gold lira left, and you, Mehmet, have a gold lira, and you, Deli—have you not a gold lira left? I have a plan. By gritting our teeth, we *could* manage to get from day to day. Suppose I manage my lira wisely and feed all three of us for a month. Mehmet, would you then care for us for another month?"

"Indeed, I would," declared Mehmet. "And we can all the time be seeking work."

"Don't forget me!" said Deli. "With my gold lira I shall help us all through the third month."

Good friend though Deli was, Ahmet and Mehmet both smiled behind their hands to think that he could help them. More than a mite foolish he was, that Deli, and a spendthrift as well, but a friend nonetheless. Allah willing, they should not have to lean upon Deli! Surely by that time, they would have found work to do.

By close figuring, Ahmet managed to support the three of them for a whole month on the single gold lira that he had. After that one month was over, Mehmet, who had gained courage from Ahmet, said, "Now *I* shall support us for one month with my one gold piece. Surely by the end of that time we shall find work to do for our bread and cheese." And Mehmet, by shopping wisely here and there, supported himself and his friends for a whole month on his single gold lira. But by the end of that month, not a one of the three friends had been able to find a job.

Now it was Deli's turn. Of course, he was determined to do as well as his friends, and to keep all three on good terms with their stomachs. But, alas, habit is worse than rabies, and from habit Deli spent on this and that small thing until in almost no time at all, his whole gold lira had been spent. The month was barely under way, and Deli felt he must keep his promise, as his friends had done.

After thinking and thinking until his empty head ached, Deli finally decided upon a plan. Without telling his friends his plan, he stretched out at full length upon the floor of his cottage and lay as still as death. Time came, time went, and at last Ahmet and Mehmet came to see what Deli planned to do about their one meal that day. Startled to find him lying motionless on the floor, they tried to revive him, but they could find no sign of life at all. Failing in this, they searched his pockets and found not a single kuruş. "Poor Deli," said Ahmet. "Here he lies, and with no money even for a decent burial! What shall we do?"

At length, they decided to wash him and wrap him in his shroud and leave him in front of the mosque. Perhaps some Moslem coming or going from the prayer service would give alms, so that Deli might be properly buried. To make certain that Deli would be helped, Mehmet pinned a note to the shroud saying, "This man is a poor man, with nobody in the world to help him. Please leave some money so that he might be carried in a coffin to the cemetery." Then they hoisted him to their shoulders and took him to the mosque and laid him out in full view of the worshipers entering the mosque courtyard.

As Ahmet and Mehmet had hoped, those who passed the body on their way to and from their prayers were moved by pity, and they left coins for the purpose of giving the dead man a decent burial. After the courtyard had become quiet, Ahmet and Mehmet came and, taking the money, they carried their friend Deli to the *imam* so that his body might be properly washed for burial. The imam took the body to an inside room in the mosque and left it there while he went to get water and soap for the washing.

While the imam was gone, Deli opened his eyes and looked about him. The first thing he saw was strings and strings of dried figs hanging here and there from the ceiling. Feeling the yawning cavern in his stomach, Deli pulled down one string of figs after another, eating them with great relish until he had filled his stomach. Then he lay down again and closed his eyes.

Shortly after that, the imam entered the room and was astonished to discover that his dried figs were gone. He looked here and there and then suddenly realized what must have happened. He bent down and opened Deli's mouth and, true enough, there were fig seeds caught between his teeth.

"Wake up, you lying corpse!" the imam shouted. "It was *you* who ate my figs. You are no more dead than I am!"

Deli lay there, for all the world as dead as a stone.

"So *that's* the way you want it!" exclaimed the imam. "Just wait and see how comfortably you will lie in the cold grave, with earth spread over your eyes. *Then* we'll see how you like this business of playing dead."

Quickly he put Deli in a coffin in a handcart and trundled him straight to the cemetery. Painstakingly he dug a grave in the gathering dark and put Deli's body inside and covered him lightly with earth. Saying to himself, "I wonder what he'll do," he hid behind a tree and waited.

Night came on, and the moon rose. Five or six shadows

appeared on the other side of the graveyard. The shadows came closer and closer. As they came nearer, the imam realized that these were six thieves who were carrying big sacks on their backs. The six men came and stopped by Deli's grave. One among them said, "Here. This is good. Nobody passing along the road can see us. Come on. Without wasting any time, let us share these treasures and then run away from here."

The thieves emptied all the contents of the sacks on the ground—clothes, gold, diamonds, and many other things. When they were all heaped together, the leader began to divide them equally: "One for you, one for you, one for you," and so on, until each had a large pile of the goods before him. Each one then took a sack and stuffed his share inside. But one object the six were unable to share, and that was a big sabre inlaid with diamonds. How could they share this? The leader of the thieves said, "I have a solution to our problem. Let's dig a newly buried person out of his grave, and whoever can divide him into three equal parts with this sabre will win the sabre." The others agreed to this proposal.

Looking around them to find a newly buried body, they noticed Deli's fresh grave. All this time, the imam, so frightened that his teeth chattered, had been watching very carefully. *"Now what will come of this?"* he wondered. As for Deli, lying in the grave and hearing what was being talked about, he said to himself, "Unless Allah intervenes, I must surely taste of death."

The thieves, after they had cast out the dirt on top of the grave with their hands, pulled Deli on up and laid him straight on the ground. Then they handed the sabre to the leader of the thieves, who came very close to where Deli was. He lifted the sabre into the air. Just as he was about to bring it down, Deli suddenly leaped to his feet and began shouting at the top of his voice, "Hey, dead bodies! All the dead, all of you, get on your feet. Get on your feet, you dead ones!"

This voice, bursting out in the night in the quiet cemetery, startled the thieves almost senseless. And the ghostlike Deli, who stood right in front of them with his white shroud gleaming in the moonlight, frightened them so that they forgot about their diamonds, gold, and other valuables. Lifting one foot after the other, they began to run as they had never run before.

The imam, doubled over with laughter, came from behind the tree where he had been hiding. He and Deli quickly gathered up the six sacks of treasure and the huge sabre. Putting them in the coffin on the imam's handcart, they carried them home to the imam's house. The next morning, as the law required, they carried the treasure in to the office of the sultan's agent and reported the whole affair. As it happened, the treasure had been stolen from the palace itself, and the sultan was so happy to have the treasure recovered that he gave Deli and the imam each three bags of gold. As for the sabre, he gave that to Deli as a prize for his courage.

As soon as Deli had left the palace, he ran to find Ahmet and Mehmet. Quickly he told them what had passed over his head since they had left him with the imam. "Look, now!" he cried, and he opened the three bags of gold that the sultan had given him. "Now we shall have food for our stomachs and clothes for our backs," he said happily. "As for this sabre, we shall keep it to frighten thieves away from our treasure!"

From that time on, Ahmet, Mehmet, and Deli lived happily and comfortably. May we all have a share of their good fortune!

Two Fools and
the Gifts for Mehmet

Once there was and twice there wasn't a young man who had nothing in the world but the clothes on his back. Seeking shelter, he came to a little cottage. *Tok, tok, tok*! He knocked at the door, and an old woman came and opened it.

"Auntie," he said, "I'm tired from walking, and I haven't had a mouthful to eat. Could you take me in for a day or so as the guest of Allah?"

The old woman looked at the shabby fellow, with his shoes worn out from walking. "Son, where have you come from? You must have traveled a long way."

"Ah, yes," said the stranger. "I've come clear from the otherworld."

"Oh, *have* you? Did you see our Mehmet there?"

"Are you Mehmet's mother? What good luck for both of us! Mehmet sent a message to you by me. He said, 'Tell my mother that I'm miserable here, with nothing decent to wear, and with absolutely no money.'"

"Oh, my poor Mehmet!" cried the woman. "Come right on in, my son; sit down and have a share of my meal. While you're eating, I'll gather some things to send to our Mehmet. Let's see . . . my husband's new suit would fit him. And of course he'll need some money. I'll fill his pockets with that. And he's always liked my bread—here's a fresh loaf."

After he had finished eating, she piled these gifts for Mehmet into the young man's arms. "Thank you *so* much for the message. And please give Mehmet our greetings—from his father and from me!" she called after the traveler as he went down the road.

Now, the young man was happy about this unexpected change in his fortunes, but he was worried, too. "What if the woman's husband comes home and finds out about all this? It could be very bad for me if he did." He ate the good loaf of bread as he hurried along—after all, he had not had enough to satisfy him at the old lady's house, and the bread cried out to be eaten. Still, he kept looking behind him for the woman's husband.

Meanwhile, the husband had come home from his fields, and he had a fine harvest of melons to take to market. "My wife," he called, "get out my new suit. I'll put it on and go to market to sell these melons right away."

"Oh!" said the wife, "I can't bring you your suit. A young man was here today from the otherworld with a message from our Mehmet. He said Mehmet needed clothes, so I sent our son your suit. In fact, I sent him some money, too."

"Are you crazy, woman?" shouted her husband. "Which way did that fellow go?"

The wife pointed down the road. Quickly the husband put on his boots, mounted his horse, and set out after the thief, *chick-a-dock, chick-a-dock, chick-a-dock.* "'Otherworld,' indeed!" he muttered as he rode.

As the young man looked back, he could see the dust rising from the road. What could he do to save himself now? Then, praise Allah!, he saw a bald-headed farmer plowing a field nearby. "Oh, father, greetings to you!" he called.

And, "Greetings to *you*, son," answered the old man.

"Father, do you see that rider coming? He's collecting bald heads for the padişah of Ankara! Quick! Climb that tree, and save your precious head!"

"He won't get *my* bald head!" said the farmer. Quickly he dropped the reins of his team of oxen and scrambled up and up into the tree. For his part, the young man tucked the new suit inside his own baggy trousers, picked up the oxen's reins, and plowed as earnestly as the farmer had.

The horseman galloped to the edge of that very field. "Greetings, son," he said to the plowman.

And "Greetings to *you*, horseman," said the "farmer," mopping his brow with his sleeve.

"There was a stranger here just now," said the horseman. "Where did he go?"

"I saw someone climbing that tree over there. Is that the stranger you're looking for?" asked the plowman.

Immediately, the horseman dismounted, ran to the tree, and pulled off his boots so he could climb more easily. The bald-headed farmer shouted, "Climb! Climb! But you won't get *my* bald head!"

And "*Keep* your bald head, for all of me, you thief!" answered the horseman. "I want my new suit back!" And, leg over leg, he made his way up the tree.

As soon as the horseman had started up the tree, the plowman dropped the oxen's reins, ran over and snatched the horseman's boots, hurriedly mounted the horse, and, *chick-a-dock, chick-a-dock, chick-a-dock*, away he rode. "Bald head!" "My new suit!" "Bald head!" "My new suit!" He could hear the shouting even over the "*chick-a-dock.*"

Well, the horseman and the bald-headed farmer both came down the tree. The farmer went back to his plow, glad that his head was safe upon his shoulders. As for the husband, after a long, long walk he reached home.

"Well," his wife asked, "did you get your new suit back again?"

"No," answered the husband. "He had forgotten the boots that Mehmet needed, and I sent those, too, along with the horse. Mehmet should be pleased to get his clothes so quickly."

Thus it was that *two* fools provided for their son Mehmet in the otherworld. And may we all be spared from such a trick as that one!

Three Tricksters
and the Pot of Butter

In a certain village there were two *köses* as much alike as two halves of the same apple. Not even their wives could tell Ahmet and Mehmet apart. What's more, in the next village there was a third köse, Hasan, who looked and walked and talked exactly like Ahmet and Mehmet.

One day Ahmet said to Mehmet, "Let's go to visit Hasan."

"Fine," said Mehmet. And away they walked to Hasan's village.

Tok, tok, tok! They knocked at Hasan's door, and, "Welcome!" he said, inviting them in.

As they talked of this and that, Hasan's wife called, "My dear, I need more butter for my cooking." And Hasan carried a huge pot of butter from the shed into the kitchen.

"Did you *see* that pot of butter?" Ahmet whispered to Mehmet.

"Yes, indeed," said Mehmet. "Let's take it with us when we go."

"And let's go early," added Ahmet.

The dinner was delicious, and the two guests ate until they could scarcely breathe. But when Hasan's wife began to lay out sleeping mats for them, Ahmet said, "Our wives are expecting us at home."

Hasan was surprised. "You're not going to stay with us tonight?"

"Next time we'll stay," Mehmet promised. "But today we came only for a short visit." And in a little while Ahmet and Mehmet set off down the path. Just out of sight, they waited quietly.

As soon as Hasan had blown out the lamp and gone to bed, Mehmet and Ahmet crept into the shed. "Here's the butter," whispered Ahmet. "I'll carry it first, and then you can carry it." And away they hurried, *pit pat pit pat.*

Meanwhile, Hasan couldn't sleep. "Strange thing," he said to his wife. "Why didn't they stay here tonight? Wife, go see if that pot of butter is safe."

His wife peered into the shed, and, "It's gone!" she cried.

"Those rascals!" exclaimed Hasan. "I'll catch them before they reach their own village." He ran after them, and soon he heard them talking.

"Here, Mehmet," said Ahmet. "You carry the pot a little way. I need to step into the woods. Walk slowly. I'll be along in a few minutes." And he handed the butter pot to Mehmet.

Hasan waited a moment or two. Then, stepping alongside Mehmet, he said, "Thank you, Mehmet. I feel better now. I'll carry the pot again."

"My, but you were quick," said Mehmet.

"I hurried so that we can get to our own village before Hasan discovers that his butter is gone," said Hasan, sounding exactly like Mehmet. "Quickly, now! And we'd better not talk for a while."

In the quiet darkness, Mehmet hurried forward, while Hasan hurried back home with his pot of butter. "Mehmet! Mehmet! Where are you?" called Ahmet. "I'll take the butter now." And he reached for the pot.

"But I've already given you the butter," said Mehmet. "I gave it to you as soon as you asked for it."

"But I didn't ask for it before," said Ahmet. "So who *does* have it?"

"Hasan!" exclaimed the two in one breath. "That rascal took his butter back home. Let's go and get it again." And back they hurried to Hasan's house.

Hasan had just tucked himself into bed when Ahmet and Mehmet stepped into the shed. "Ah, here it is," whispered Mehmet. "This time I'll carry it first." And this time they hurried twice as fast down the path.

Meanwhile, Hasan couldn't sleep and he *couldn't* sleep. "I'll go out and see if the butter is still there," he said. When he reached the shed, "Aman!" he cried. "Those scamps have taken our butter again. There's nothing to do but to go after it."

Down the path he went after Ahmet and Mehmet and the pot of butter, all the way to the two köses' village. As Hasan passed the village guest house, he heard voices. Ahmet and Mehmet had stopped there to divide the butter.

"We can't divide it evenly without weighing it," said Ahmet. "Mehmet, go to Ali's house and borrow some scales. His lamp is still on." Mehmet went to borrow Ali's scales.

While Mehmet was gone, Hasan came in. "Ali and his wife had visitors," he said, "so I didn't ask for the scales. Why don't you go to Ruhi's house and borrow his scales?"

"All right," said Ahmet.

As soon as Ahmet had left, Hasan picked up the butter and, *patur kitur patur kitur,* carried it back to his own house. This time he put it right by his bed. "Now *I'll* sleep soundly, and so will the butter," he said.

Meanwhile, Ahmet and Mehmet both came back to the village guest house. Ahmet had a pair of scales, and Mehmet had a pair of scales. "You sent me to get scales from Ruhi's house," said Ahmet. "Why did you get some, too?"

"But you sent me first to borrow scales from Ali," said Mehmet, "and here they are."

"You said Ali had visitors," said Ahmet. "Then you sent me to get scales from Ruhi."

Mehmet shook his head. "I came back just now," he said slowly. "Do you suppose . . ."

"Hasan!" they both said in the same breath.

"It was *Hasan* who came in. And he took the pot of butter. He's as slippery as the butter in that pot!" said Ahmet.

"Yes, this time we were outtricked," Mehmet agreed. "But at least we made him run to keep his own butter!" Laughing, and clapping each other on the shoulder, Ahmet and Mehmet went home to their beds.

As for that butter, it made many delicious dishes at clever Hasan's house. I know, for I ate one there myself the night he told me this story.

Trousers Mehmet and
the Sultan's Daughter

Once there was and twice there wasn't a clever village boy named Mehmet. When his old father died, leaving him nothing but a pair of baggy trousers and his blessing, Mehmet stored the blessing in his heart. Then, putting the trousers over his shoulder, he set one foot before the other till he came to İstanbul.

"No work, no bread," thought he. "Though I can read, I've learned no trade, so I shall carry burdens to earn my keep. And since I have neither basket nor rope, these trousers must serve as my sack."

A kind old tailor sewed the trouser legs shut. Then, "*Hamal*! Porter!" he shouted. "Let Trousers Mehmet carry your bundles!"

"Trousers Mehmet, here's a package!" Soon Mehmet's cheerful face appeared in shops and markets throughout the city, and he had work a-plenty.

One day just as he left Sirkeci Station carrying a heavy load, he saw a splendid procession on its way from Topkapı Palace to the Covered Bazaar. In a golden litter sat the sultan's daughter, with her merry brown eyes smiling at him above her veil.

"Ah, how I could love that lady!" sighed Mehmet as he watched. "But she's far too fine to love a poor hamal like me."

As for the princess, the handsome hamal had touched her heart. "*There* is a young man who truly pleases me," she murmured. "But what can bring a princess and a porter together?"

Amid the bustle and the chatter of the Covered Bazaar, the princess thought long and longer about Trousers Mehmet. Suddenly she had an idea.

The next morning, she went before the sultan. "Father, is it not time for me to be married?" she asked.

"Married!" he exclaimed. "For two years, young men have come seeking your hand. But would you choose one? Not at all!"

"Father, none of them was *half* as clever as you," she said, "and therefore none of them would do."

"And how am I to find such a clever young man?" asked the sultan, pleased by his daughter's compliment.

"You could set a task so difficult that only the cleverest of men could complete it," she suggested.

The sultan considered the matter. Then, "Yes, my daughter," he decided. "I shall send envoys to every kingdom inviting princes to compete for my daughter's hand."

"Only princes, Father?" she asked. "It is not only princes who are clever."

"You are right, my daughter," he agreed. And, true enough, criers were sent out immediately shouting, "Come! Come! Whoever seeks to wed the princess must come to Topkapı Palace!"

Within three or five days, young men of every shape and size and station had gathered at the palace. Even Trousers Mehmet joined the throng. He loved the princess already, and no one had said that hamals could not try for her hand.

Looking directly at the suitors, the sultan himself announced, "The man who wins my daughter must bring to me one who hunts, who throws away what he catches, and who carries with him what he cannot find."

The suitors stared at one another. Who could make sense of such a task as that? Clearly, the sultan had lost his wits. One by one, they turned away, except for Trousers Mehmet. He stood there, thinking. The sultan was said to be a clever man. Perhaps this was a riddle . . . not one to be found in books, but on the lips of the people.

As Mehmet went out slowly into the busy street, the *muezzin* called from a minaret of Sultan Ahmet mosque. "It is time for noonday prayer," said Mehmet. "After that, I shall think about the sultan's task."

He hurried to Ablutions Fountain in the mosque yard. There he washed himself three times. Then, leaving his shoes at the mosque door, he went inside to pray.

As Mehmet passed a public fountain after the holy service,

he saw a wretched peasant making himself clean. His washing done, the peasant set about that unpleasant bit of business known to the poor the world over.

Mehmet smiled. Then suddenly his heart pounded, *tum tum tum*. Was this by any chance the kind of hunter the sultan meant? He went to the peasant. "Brother," he said, "if you will come with me for half an hour, I shall buy your bread and cheese for three or five days."

The peasant stared at Mehmet. "Empty words do not fill an empty stomach," he grumbled. Then, as Mehmet still stood there, he said, "First I must finish what I am doing, son. Then I shall come."

"If you wish the bread and cheese, you must come now," said Mehmet. "You may finish what you are doing when we reach Topkapı Palace."

"The sultan's palace!" exclaimed the peasant. "Indeed not! My life is worth more to me than bread and cheese. Still, my father used to say that it's better to die on a full stomach than to live on an empty one . . ."

"Fear not," said Mehmet. "Only trust me, and you will see. Come." And he and the peasant went directly to the palace.

Immediately, they were taken to the sultan. The ruler stared at Mehmet curiously. A hamal . . . with an old pair of trousers for a basket! And he had a ragged peasant with him, itching and scratching. "Well," said the sultan, "what is your business here?"

"This morning, sire," said Mehmet, "you set a task for the man who wished to wed your daughter. I have brought the hunter you described." Then, turning to the peasant, Mehmet said, "Now, brother, you may finish that business you began at the fountain."

Obediently, the peasant began to search among his tattered clothes for lice. As he found a louse, he would flatten it on his thumbnail and then throw it away. One, two, three, four, five—and still he scratched.

"Enough!" said the sultan, smiling a little despite himself.

"Well, sire," asked Mehmet, "have I not brought to you one who hunts, who throws away what he catches, and who carries with him what he cannot find?"

"You have," agreed the sultan.

"Praise be to Allah!" said Mehmet happily. And from his worn purse, he gave the peasant a handful of coins. "Eat with a hearty appetite, brother," he said, "and thank you. May your way be open." The peasant left, pleased with this strange bargain.

"Now," said Mehmet eagerly, "when may I marry your daughter?"

The sultan's eyes glittered coldly. "Not so fast," he warned. "I do not intend to have my daughter marry a hamal."

"But, sire," Mehmet said, "you promised . . ."

"I know," interrupted the sultan angrily. "But how could I guess that a *porter* would seek her hand? Naturally, a hamal would be well acquainted with lice! No, you cannot have my daughter, unless . . . unless you succeed in a second task, and then a third. *Then* you may have my daughter."

Mehmet swallowed his anger and disappointment. "Very well, sire," he said. "What is the second task?"

The sultan thought for a moment. Then he replied, "You must bring me life which enters an empty box alone, yet comes out bringing death with it."

Mehmet's shoulders sagged, but he bowed and left the sultan's presence. "Fair or unfair, he is nonetheless the sultan," the hamal murmured, "and the father of the lovely princess. Thorns and roses surely grow on the same tree! Still, Allah willing, I shall win the sultan's daughter."

He straightened his shoulders and went directly to the Covered Bazaar. "At least," he decided, "I can buy a box while I am thinking."

He searched among the stalls until he found a small wooden box with a snug cover. Paying the shopkeeper, he tucked the box into his sash.

As he was leaving the Bazaar, he heard the *boom-boom-boom* of a drum and the mellow piping of a *zurna*. "Come and see!" a showman sang, and the crowd hurried to his stall. "Wonders from India." "Wonders from China." "See something you have never seen before—a miracle!" Mehmet read the bold signs above the stall.

For a moment forgetting his own problem, Mehmet smiled.

"Man is truly as old as his head, not his years. Just see the crowd scramble!"

Suddenly he noticed something special. "From Egypt," the sign said. As he reached out to touch what he saw, the showman shouted, "Take your hands off that cage. There's *trouble* inside."

"I'll pay you well for just *half* of that trouble," said Mehmet quietly, and reached into his sash for his box and his purse.

"Do you know what you are buying?" asked the showman.

"I know what I am buying," answered Mehmet. Carefully, carefully . . . in a moment, Mehmet had a small something in his box. And the showman had a large sum in his purse.

With his joy shortening his journey, Mehmet was soon at the palace. "Well," asked the sultan, "have you brought life in a box?"

"Yes, sire, and it brings death with it when it leaves the box," replied Trousers Mehmet. "Here it is."

The sultan turned the box over and over. Then he laughed. "You are bold, young man, but how can you prove what you say? There is no way of seeing into that box of yours. Open it."

"As you say, sire," said Mehmet politely, and he lifted the cover just enough so that the sultan could see the gleaming eyes of a deadly asp.

"Shut it!" the sultan cried. And Mehmet shut the box.

"Well, sire," said Mehmet, smiling, "I have accomplished the second task. What is the third task to be?"

The sultan stared at the young hamal. Then slowly he drew forth his own silken handkerchief. Holding it out to Mehmet, he said, "Bring me a thousand forests in this handkerchief."

Mehmet took the handkerchief and slipped it safely into his sash. He studied the sultan's face, but it gave no hint of the answer. Had he come within a hair of winning his princess only to lose her on this puzzling task? Still, he kept the small bird of hope alive within his breast.

"This may be another riddle," he mused as he left the palace and walked along the winding streets and through the main gate into Gülhane Park. As he wandered along a shady path, he murmured, "I begin with the name of Allah. A thousand forests . . ." Suddenly there was a snapping sound beneath his foot. He moved his shoe, and—Allah be praised!—there lay an answer to the puzzle.

He picked up another just like the one he had crushed. Rolling the treasure inside the sultan's handkerchief, he tucked it gently into his sash. Then he hurried back to the palace.

"Well," said the ruler, "have you *hidden* the forests somewhere? I cannot see even the handkerchief."

"Here, sire," answered Trousers Mehmet, drawing it carefully from his sash. The sultan stared curiously as Mehmet unrolled the handkerchief and took out a single acorn.

A broad smile spread across the sultan's face. Who could deny that Allah proposed a thousand forests from that one acorn? And, indeed, who could doubt that Allah proposed this clever young man as a husband fit for the sultan's daughter?

Thus it was that Trousers Mehmet came to marry the sultan's daughter, in a wedding that lasted forty days and forty nights. May we all have a share in their happiness!

Riddles

We pay for it and get it, but others get it from our hand
without even paying for it. What is it?

(Ticket)

Open-mouthed see the monster sit,
With red-hot doomsday inside it!
(Oven)

When it's C, to O it turns,
Then from O to C returns.
(Moon)

Stargazer to the Sultan

O nce there was and once there wasn't, when yesterday was today and the sieve lay in the hay—well, in those times there was an old woodcutter who lived at the edge of a village. Every day he trudged off to the forest, a stout rope and an axe over one shoulder and a bit of bread and cheese in a string bag over the other. In the morning, *chut-chut-chut*, he chopped, and in the afternoon, "Wood! Wood! Wood!" he cried, selling his bundle in the marketplace. Allah willing, the woodcutter earned a few kuruş, enough to buy for himself and his wife a loaf of bread, an onion, a cutting of cheese, and three or five olives.

Life would have rolled on year after year in this manner if his wife had been content. But, alas, she dreamed only of being rich. As fate would have it, she was passing the hamam one day with her water pitcher when a handsome carriage drew up before the bathhouse. Out stepped a woman with a dress so beautiful and gems so glittering that the woodcutter's wife could scarcely trust her own senses. She gaped as three serving maids followed the woman into the bath, carrying her parcels of towels and sweetmeats and elegant clean clothing. As soon as the bathhouse door had closed behind them, she tugged at the sleeve of the hamam keeper. "Who *is* she?" she whispered.

"Oh, don't you know?" he exclaimed. "She is the wife of the sultan's chief stargazer."

"A stargazer," she mused as she filled her pitcher at the village fountain. "My husband, too, must become a stargazer to the sultan. Then *I* shall go here and there in beautiful gowns and jingle with jewels and have servants to follow me, bearing my bundles."

From the moment her husband entered the cottage that evening, he heard little but stargazer, stargazer. "You must become an astrologer to the sultan," the woman insisted, with her husband all the while staring at her as if she had mislaid her wits. "Surely you want me to live in a beautiful house and have fine dresses and wear jewels at my throat. Look! Just *look* at these patches on patches I am wearing!"

Finally, when she had stopped for a moment to catch her breath, "My wife," he said patiently, "how am I to become a stargazer to the sultan? Of *course* I should like to have you live in a beautiful house and to own all the lovely things that women long for. But I am such a poor grasshopper of a man that I can barely keep us in bread and cheese. Who would even *dream* that I could become an astrologer? Pray, wife, be content with what is at hand. After all, we have our own cottage, and enough to eat, and clothing for our backs."

But, indeed, who could make such a woman listen to reason? She kept after the poor man and *after* him, with the woodcutter all the while saying, "Oh, my dear, how can I? How can you ask such a thing of me?" At length, being a good-hearted man and fond of his wife, he agreed at least to think about the matter.

A few days later, the woodcutter's wife was wakened by the voice of the town crier, shouting street by street and alleyway by alleyway, "Lost! Lost! The sultan's daughter has lost her most valuable ring. Reward! Reward! The sultan offers a handsome reward for the finder of the ring."

"Get up! Get up, my husband!" called the woodcutter's wife. "Here is the chance we have been seeking. Go at once to the sultan and tell him you are an astrologer of special power and can find the ring belonging to his daughter. If you are successful, we can lead a rich and full life. Go. And do not come back into this house until you have become a stargazer to the sultan."

Many years of his wife's nimble tongue had been sample enough to tell the woodcutter that here he faced a road which had no turning. "I begin with the name of Allah," he murmured, and, trembling from nose to toes, he put one foot before the other until he had arrived at the sultan's gate. There he announced himself as a new astrologer, come to find the missing ring. Immediately, he was led into the presence of the sultan himself. "Understand, astrologer, that if you find the ring you will be richly rewarded. If you *fail*, the loss of your head must pay the price of your bad judgment," the sultan declared, marveling that this mere mite of a man could possess such remarkable powers.

"Ah, sire, I *do* understand," the woodcutter answered. "I have but one request, if you will be pleased to grant it."

"Yes, yes? And what is that?"

"I must be left alone for forty days and forty nights, forty nights in which to study Allah's handiwork in the stars and forty days in which to deliberate upon His mercies. At the end of that time, Allah willing, the truth will be revealed." The little woodcutter knew all too well the only truth that would be known at the close of his watching and waiting: that his claim had been beyond his power to fulfill.

The sultan pondered. Then, "Since my own astrologers—even my chief stargazer—have been unable to promise as much, you may *have* your forty days and forty nights," the sultan agreed. Calling his most trusted servant, the ruler had the woodcutter taken to a room with one wide window near the ceiling. The key was turned in the lock, and the poor woodcutter was left alone with his thoughts.

Day after day he paced the flagstone floor; night after night he watched the endless procession of the stars. But what truth could *stars* tell a simple woodcutter except that he was indeed no astrologer at all? Long as he might look at the stars, his gazing would discover no ring. It would serve only to remind him of the insignificance of such a grasshopper as he in the eyes of Allah.

Each day the sultan's favorite servant came to bring food to the woodcutter. Wonderful food it was, too, straight from the sultan's table. But in the face of such a fate as his, the woodcutter had no stomach for food. For him, these fine meals brought but a single comfort: a certain way of counting the passing of the days until the sultan must learn the truth which now rested heavily on the heart of the new astrologer. Each evening, just before the servant came to carry away the tray, the poor woodcutter removed one small plate and added it to the pile growing all too quickly in the corner of the room, each time murmuring to himself, "Thirty more days, and then the sultan will know," or "Twenty-nine more days, and then the sultan will know."

Now, in fact, a great fear had been growing in the heart of the servant. For it was he himself who had stolen the ring belonging to the sultan's daughter. Coming and going, he had one day seen his opportunity and, trusting he would remain unsuspected, he had slipped the ring into the lining of his sleeve. As the time for the stargazer's deliberations drew to a close, the servant chanced to overhear the new astrologer murmuring, "Three more days, and then the sultan will know." Certain that his secret had been discovered, he decided that the only hope for his desperate case rested in the hands of the little stargazer, clearly a kindhearted man despite his remarkable wisdom.

The next evening, instead of merely handing the tray inside, the servant carried it into the room and set it down in its place upon the floor. Then, closing the door and locking it from the inside, he sank to his knees before the dumbfounded woodcutter. "Please, sire," he begged, "listen to my story, the tale of a wretched man indeed. Then, if Allah move your heart to do so, help me!" With his eyes flowing like two fountains in his anxiety and grief, he poured forth the account of his theft, sparing not a single detail. "You said last evening, 'Only three more days, and then the sultan will know,'" he concluded. "Now there are only *two* days left before the truth will be revealed. Allah be praised, you, good sire, will never feel the pain one heedless act can bring. How can you, at once a wise and innocent man, know the torment of sleepless nights and the anguish of joyless days that have been mine? But, sire, you *do* know this: If the sultan learns of my guilt, I shall lose not only my bread and my bed, but my head! Please, sire, have pity upon me. Do not tell the sultan of my misdeed. I shall do anything—*anything*—if only you will save me from the fate that lies in store for me when the truth becomes known."

For the first time in thirty-eight days, the little woodcutter drew a comfortable breath. Allah alone had spared him, this small grasshopper of a man. And could he himself fail to pity the trembling one still kneeling before him? Grasping the servant by the hands, he gazed into his eyes. "Fear not. Allah willing, I shall take care of the matter in such a fashion that the sultan will never know who stole the ring. The *truth* will not be known, but the ring will be found. There is one thing, and one thing only, that you must do. On the morrow, buy in the marketplace a pure black cock, one with not a single fleck or feather lighter than midnight. While the other household servants are still at prayer, add this cock to the flock in the sultan's poultry yard. On the fortieth day, force the black cock to swallow a bit of dough containing the ring. Then leave the rest to me. If you do exactly as I have said, I shall not reveal your secret to the sultan."

Earnestly promising to do as the woodcutter had directed, the grateful servant arose, unlocked the door, and left the room. As for the woodcutter, suddenly he had found his appetite, and he ate all the foods brought from the sultan's table, his heart each moment singing with relief and joy.

Very early on the morning of the forty-first day, the sultan ordered the servant to lead the new astrologer into his presence. Assured that all had been made ready, the woodcutter walked confidently into the room where the sultan awaited him.

"Well, you have had the forty days and forty nights which you requested," the sultan began. "Now, where is the ring?"

"I shall show you the ring in the courtyard today before the call for noontime prayers," the woodcutter answered. "Meanwhile, please summon to appear before you just inside the courtyard gate every person in your household, of whatever rank, from the highest official to the lowliest servant. In addition, cause to be brought to the gate every animal belonging to you and within your palace grounds—dogs, cats, horses, cattle, poultry—all living creatures, that they may pass in procession before you. Allah willing, the ring will be revealed."

Curious indeed to discover how the woodcutter would detect the thief, the sultan sent criers to summon his entire household. First in procession came the women, from the highest to the lowest, from those richly attired to those in patches, all heavily veiled. Not a word of accusation passed the lips of the new astrologer, and the women returned to their own quarters in the harem and elsewhere about their business.

Next, beginning with the grand vizier, came the officials, splendidly dressed. These were closely followed by all the male servants whose work lay within the confines of the palace wall. Making proper obeisance before the ruler, they passed in solemn, silent procession. Still no sign of accusation came from the stargazer, and the men left the presence of the sultan, to engage in whispered wonderings about the guilty one.

At last came the animals, one by one, some mute and some in protest against this strange turn of affairs. Suddenly the astrologer spoke. "Sire, yonder struts a black cock. Have him seized and killed. Within his crop you will find the ring you seek."

Immediately, the cock was caught and carried to the sultan. It was but the matter of a moment to relieve the cock at once of his breath and of his burden. And, as the woodcutter had declared, within the crop gleamed the ring belonging to the sultan's daughter.

Turning to the woodcutter, the sultan announced, "You must now have the reward you so justly deserve for your services. I pronounce you an official stargazer to the sultan. As soon as you wish, you may move with your household into the small palace just outside my gate. There you will lead a rich and full life."

The dazed woodcutter, after taking proper leave of the sultan, hurried home to tell his wife the outcome of his labors. Since the two had little or nothing of value to carry with them, they readied themselves in no time at all to enter the splendid home that was now theirs. Day after day, the wife preened herself before her mirror, trying on one new dress after another, and feasting her eyes upon the gems given to her at the sultan's command. Servants scurried here and there, and none could be prouder than the woodcutter's wife as she sent them about their business. What could be more to her taste than such a life as this?

As for the little woodcutter, day after day he sat in idleness, his brain a-scramble and his throat a-tip-tap with anxiety. For who could tell what service might next be required of him by the sultan? The more accustomed his wife became to their new life, the less comfortable the old woodcutter felt. All too soon, these things could be snatched away, and what pleasure could such borrowed splendor bring an honest heart?

One day as the woodcutter sat meditating alone in their garden, his wife ran to him in great agitation. "My dear," she cried, "you must *do* something. I cannot go on any longer in this poor fashion!"

Staring at his wife, the woodcutter replied, "*What* poor fashion? It seems to me that we are living in very *fine* fashion. A short time ago, we praised Allah daily for the meager life we shared in our cottage. Surely we should be even more grateful for this elegant home in which we dwell. Just see how lovely you look in your new gowns. And note the glitter of gold at your throat. How can you call *this* poor fashion?"

"Ah," she sighed, "until today I felt fortunate. But this morning I discovered that the *chief* stargazer to the sultan has a kiosk within the palace wall itself. His wife wears dresses far more beautiful than mine, and her gems make mine look paltry indeed. I am no longer satisfied, my dear. You must become the sultan's chief stargazer. Then I shall be happy."

"Oh, my wife, let not your heart be troubled by envy," he urged. "Such luxury is not needful for us. Please be content with what we have."

But it is easier to make a camel jump a ditch than to make a fool listen to reason. The wife would not accept anything less than the life offered in that kiosk within the palace wall. "Go," she said. "And do not expect a meal under this roof until you have become chief stargazer to the sultan."

Head in hands, the little woodcutter considered his dilemma. Being a sensible man, he valued his life far more than an elegant roof above his head. This house they had was quite fine enough for him, and in time his wife must learn to accept it as the best that he could give her. Well he knew the risk of further venture as a stargazer. Far from wishing to become chief stargazer to the sultan, the humble woodcutter desired freedom from even his present official post. As long as he must dwell in dread, no roof could truly shelter him, be it humble or fine.

Suddenly he was struck by a plan at once so simple and so sound that he resolved to act upon it. Since the sultan considered his astrologers beyond question men of wisdom, one who appeared the most fantastic of fools could scarcely be thought worthy of such a title. The new astrologer must merely behave as one who had entirely lost his wits, so that he could no longer be relied on as an astrologer. Relieved of his position, he could then truly enjoy the comfortable life which his first venture had miraculously brought him.

Waiting that afternoon until the palace courtyard had ceased to buzz with its midday activity, he tucked up his robe, set his turban askew, and rushed about here and there within the palace grounds, shouting, "The sultan! The sultan! Who has seen the sultan? Quickly! Quickly! Something must be done at *once.*"

Officials and servants ran toward him from all directions. "*Hush*, man. Are you mad? What are you doing, shouting thus when the household is at rest? What can you be *thinking* of?"

But the woodcutter refused to answer their questions, crying again and again, "The sultan! Where *is* he?"

At last a servant reported that the sultan was in the bath and must not be disturbed.

"Disturbed, eh!" shouted the woodcutter. "He will be disturbed indeed when the roof of his hamam tumbles in upon his head! I *must* see the sultan at once."

Immediately, the new astrologer was seized by two of the sultan's bodyguard. "The man has surely taken leave of his senses," one declared. "There is not a stouter roof in the whole kingdom than the dome above the sultan's hamam!" And they struggled to lead the distraught woodcutter away.

Meanwhile, above the music and splashing of the bath the sultan had heard the crazed shouting in the hall, and, hastily wrapping himself in a large towel, he emerged into the corridor to confront the culprit. No sooner had the last of his towel trailed through the doorway when with a thundering crash the roof of the hamam fell in, leaving the bath a ruin.

Weak with shock and disbelief, the sultan staggered against his new astrologer, who was of all men the most amazed at the sudden crumbling of the dome. "Ah, my stargazer," babbled the sultan, "no man of ordinary powers could have foreseen such a calamity. By your wisdom you have saved my life. For this singular service, I pronounce you chief stargazer to the sultan."

Amazed at the outcome of his plan, the woodcutter went home to tell his wife what had happened. She was almost delirious with delight, and hastily gathered together the things she considered light in weight but heavy in value. As for the rest, they could be left behind. For would the two not have far more elegant quarters within the wall of the sultan's own palace? There a splendid kiosk awaited them, with far more servants, and enough dresses and diamonds to gratify even the most demanding of women. In short, the woodcutter's wife was at last satisfied.

Alas for the woodcutter, however, as the complaints of his wife were swallowed up in her content, the demands of the sultan grew in number. Oh, the anxious little astrologer had been asked no further questions. But as chief stargazer, he was expected to be at all times in the sultan's presence—at the sultan's meals, during his rides throughout the countryside, even on his strolls through the palace gardens. Another man might have relished such opportunities, might have basked in such glories. The heart of the little woodcutter was not as that of other men. For himself he would never have sought such dizzying heights. Well he knew that a single misstep could plunge him into the direst of misfortunes. The slender legs of such a grasshopper as he were not meant to carry him to this high post. One day, he was certain, all would be lost. Thus he sat silent throughout the grand dinners, and mused while others made much of their nearness to the sultan.

Noting this, the sultan thought one day to tease his chief stargazer out of his musings. As they strolled down the garden paths that evening, suddenly the sultan reached out and scooped up something into his hand. Holding his closed hand before the astrologer, he said, "You have remarkable powers, indeed. Before all these members of my court I shall prove your powers. Within my hand I hold a small something. If you can tell me what it is, I shall grant whatever you wish. It is within my power to give you what you ask. Is it within your power to tell me what I hold thus helpless within my hand?"

Here was the moment the woodcutter had been dreading. And he had no answer ready. Whatever he had scooped up out of the garden, the sultan held within his hand the life of a poor little grasshopper of a man, stargazer only by strange leaps of fortune.

In despair, the old woodcutter responded with a village proverb: "You jump once, grasshopper, and you survive. You jump twice, grasshopper, and still you live. But the third time you jump, you are caught." And he waited before the sultan. He had offered in a proverb the truth of his own life, and beyond it he knew no truth at all.

The sultan, opening his hand, revealed—a grasshopper. "You see?" he said, turning to his courtiers. "Here is a man with remarkable powers indeed, powers beyond those of ordinary men, powers that lie in the spangled heavens above. Now, my chief stargazer, ask what you will, and it shall be granted."

His heart light, his soul filled with relief and joy, the woodcutter answered, "Allah be praised, I have been able to serve your needs, my sultan. What I wish is simply this: I should like no longer to be your stargazer. I want merely to live comfortably and to meditate upon the mercies of Allah."

"Your wish will be granted," the sultan declared. "The kiosk within my palace wall is yours. And you may come and go within my kingdom as you will. But I relieve you at this hour of your title as stargazer to the sultan. Go in peace, and may your way be open."

Thus it was that the little woodcutter was enabled to dwell happily with his wife within the wall of the sultan's palace, with stomach for his food, and with eyes always for the stars, those endless reminders of the care of Allah for even one small grasshopper of a man.

The Bird of Fortune

Once there was and once there wasn't, when fleas were porters and camels were barbers—well, in that time there was a padişah who had three sons. This padişah seemed a man with only half a brain between his ears. Day after day he did foolish things, things unbecoming to his age and his position as a padişah. Caring little for the business of governing the land, he spent all his time going hunting, or engaging in other sports and entertainments.

One day, feeling in a particularly playful mood, he called his three sons to his side. "Tell me," he said. "How much do you love me?"

The princes by now were quite accustomed to their father's strange behavior, and they thought little of his question. But well they knew how angry he became when he was not answered, so answer they must.

The oldest prince spoke first. "Dear father, I love you as much as I love gold and silver and diamonds," said he.

His oldest son's answer pleased the padişah. "Well spoken!" he cried. "You must indeed love me dearly." Then he looked at his middle son. "Well, how much do *you* love me?"

The second son answered, "My dear father, I love you as much as I love honey, *börek*, and sweet pastries."

"Ah, yes, my stout son," the padişah chuckled. "If you love me in that measure, you must truly love me very much." Finally he turned to his youngest son. "Tell me, my littlest son. How much do *you* love me?"

The youngest son did not answer at once. Then, swallowing

hard, he said softly, "My dear father, I love you as much as I love salt."

This unexpected answer made his brothers shake with laughter. But the padişah's face of a sudden became cloudy. His eyebrows came together in a dark scowl, and, "What? What did you say?" he cried. "You love me as much as *salt*, eh? You faithless son! Could you not find something dearer than salt?"

Trembling with fury, he took two gold pieces from the small mother-of-pearl chest at his side. One he gave to his eldest son and the other he presented to his middle son. "Go now," he said. "In you I am well pleased, my beloved sons." Respectfully the two walked backwards from the room, bowing almost to the floor as they left.

As soon as they had gone, the padişah clapped his hands twice. When a servant entered the room, "Quickly! Call the court executioners!" he ordered.

The servant immediately ran to do his bidding. In three or five minutes, two large, frightful-looking executioners came in. The padişah, pointing to his littlest son, said, "Hurry! Take him away. Cut off his head! If you do not satisfy my order, I shall have you cut up into small pieces."

As did everybody else in the palace, both of the executioners loved the little prince dearly. But obeying the padişah's order, they grasped him by the arms and carried him from the room. Quickly they ordered two horses prepared for riding. One executioner took the little prince beside him on his horse. Then, mixing smoke with dust, they rode with great speed for the forest. At a place in the mountains far removed from the palace, they stopped. The little prince looked at them wide-eyed, awaiting his fate at their hands.

Gazing at him, the executioners were moved to pity. One said, "My dear prince, we cannot kill you. But you have heard our padişah's order. He will not be satisfied without proof of your death. Come, take off your shirt and give it to us. We shall catch and kill a hare, and dip your shirt in the blood of the hare. Then we shall say, 'Here, my padişah. We have cut the prince into two pieces!' And we shall give the bloody shirt to your father. But, for your part, you must get away from your father's land and you must never return."

The little prince immediately took off his shirt. Giving it to the executioners, he thanked them again and again for sparing his life. Taking one of the horses, he mounted and rode beyond sight into the distance.

He went a little; he went far. He went straight over hills and over rills, until finally he came to a city in another country. He was so tired that his body was all one ache, but he dismounted and knocked at the door of the first house by the side of the road.

An old woman opened the door. "My mother," the boy began, "will you be so kind as to take me in? I have nobody at all in the world to care for me. I am a stranger to this country. Please accept me as a son."

Now, as it happened, the old woman herself had no one in this world to call her own. Feeling happy that at last she could have a son, she accepted the prince willingly. While the old woman prepared food to put before him, the boy hurried to the neighborhood fountain and washed his hands, his face, and his feet. Then he returned and satisfied his stomach with the good plain food. After feeding his horse and bedding him down in the old woman's stable, the boy lay down on the straw mat that the old woman had prepared, and he fell into a deep sleep.

Not many days after that, the boy awoke one morning to the sound of carts and horses passing by the old woman's house, all going toward the center of the city. "What is this, my mother?" he called. "Is today a holiday in the city? Where is everyone going?"

The old woman answered, "No, my son, it is not a holiday. It is something much more important than that. Yesterday our padişah died. Today his viziers will set free the bird of fortune, and it will choose our new padişah."

"Oh, my dear mother," the prince cried, "*please* take me, too. We can at least watch."

The old woman was in truth eager herself to see the choice made by the bird of fortune, so she agreed to take the boy. Hurriedly they dressed themselves and went out into the street. With the crowd, they went to the meeting place at the big central square of the city. After everybody had gathered, the viziers released the bird of fortune. The bird started to fly in great circles above the crowd. Some said, "I wonder if he'll land on me?" feeling very much excited. And others said, "Oh, that he would land on *my* head!" and stood on tiptoe to make themselves taller. Meanwhile the bird flew 'round and 'round, until he came at last and perched on the head of the young prince. Immediately there were words from every mouth in the crowd. "No! He's a stranger!" "He can't be our king!" Since there appeared no other solution, the viziers announced that the next morning there would be another choice made by the bird of fortune. And so the crowd scattered.

The next day, everyone gathered again in the city square. This time, to be sure he would not arouse the anger of the crowd, the little prince went along a side street to the cemetery and sat there on a stone by the gate. Again the viziers set the bird of fortune free. The crowd was almost bursting with excitement, but there was no voice or echo from anyone. All eyes were gazing upward, following the flight of the bird. Going hither and yon, it settled at last on the head of the young prince. Again the crowd shouted its anger and disapproval. "No, no! This won't do at all!" some said. And "The chances of a Turk are three!" others cried. Therefore, the viziers announced a third trial for the following day.

The next morning, every person able to totter came very early to the public square. The prince and the old woman had just barely gone out of their house and were walking toward the crowd when the bird of fortune was set free. The bird flew over the heads of the crowd and then, going farther away, for the third time he landed on the head of the young prince. This time, the crowd must accept the choice, and they came forward one by one to greet their new padişah. On that day, the little prince began to rule his new country.

Being a clever young man, in a short time he had the whole country won over to him, and he did many fine things for his people. The news went from mouth to mouth that he governed the country like a rose. As for the little prince, he was very happy.

Several years passed over his head. At last the young padişah, without making his own identity known, sent a letter to his father inviting him to visit his country. His father, who still enjoyed all kinds of recreation and activity, accepted this invitation at once and with a group of soldiers he set forth to visit. The young padişah went with a splendid retinue to meet the visitors, and he watched anxiously for some sign of recognition from his father. But since the young king had let his beard and moustache grow, and had besides gained much in stateliness, his father never suspected that this was the son he had condemned to death for his want of judgment.

Now, the young padişah had ordered his cooks to prepare many elegant foods and meats, but to prepare them entirely without salt. The visitor and his party sat down to dinner with the greatest of expectations. But what was this? The food was without savor. Delicious as it looked, it could not please the taste without salt. His stomach faint from disappointment and hunger, the visiting padişah at length left the table, intending to look in upon his soldiers before they went to their night's rest. As he entered their quarters, all he could hear was a grumbling about the food they had been served. "Without salt!" exclaimed one. "Who ever heard of a meal without salt?" The padişah shared their dissatisfaction, but he said nothing at all about the matter to the young ruler.

The following day while they sat at the splendid but saltless noonday meal, the guest king said, "My good friend, have you no salt in your land?"

The young king answered, "Ah, indeed we do, my king, and so abundant is it that most of the salt for the whole world is sent in the ships from our own harbor here."

The visiting king was speechless with surprise. At last, piqued by curiosity, he said, "Well, but all of your meals are saltless. Whatever is the reason for serving them without salt?"

This time the young king looked puzzled. "Sire, I understood you had no taste for salt, that you held it worthless, and that you therefore never used it in your meals. In order to please you, I ordered that no salt be used in the meals in my palace during your visit."

"Impossible!" cried the old king. "Whoever told you such nonsense is a fool. How can life *be* without salt? I love salt very much indeed."

"But," said the young padişah, "when your youngest son

said he loved you as much as he loved salt, you were so angry that you put his life into the hands of your court executioners. How can that be?"

Aroused, the visiting king looked deep into the eyes of the young padişah and at last he knew the truth. This young ruler was his own son. His eyes flowing like two fountains in his joy, the old king embraced his son. "Truly," said he, "if I am as dear to you as salt, I must be dear indeed. And may Allah preserve both your love and your wisdom."

Thus it was that the two were reconciled and dwelt happily ever after. And may we have a share of their good fortune.

The Princess and the Pig

O nce there was and once there wasn't a padişah who had three daughters, each one more beautiful than the one before. One morning as he set off for town, the padişah asked, "What shall I get for you at the market?"

His oldest daughter said, "Please bring me a golden gown, Father."

His second daughter said, "Please bring me a silver sash, Father."

The youngest daughter said nothing at all.

"Well, daughter?" asked the padişah, smiling at her, for she was his favorite.

"Nothing at all, Father," she answered.

"Come, now, my daughter. Ask for whatever you want most."

"Well, then, Father, you may bring me

> Grapes that speak,
> Apples that smile,
> And apricots that tinkle in the breeze."

Her father smiled, but the older girls laughed aloud. Their sister *was* an odd one.

As for the padişah, he climbed into his carriage and drove off to the market. He found the golden gown and the silver sash easily enough. He found grapes a-plenty, but none that spoke. He found apples in heaps, but none that smiled. He found apricots by the dozens, but none that tinkled in the breeze.

He looked through the market again and again, and *still* he could not find what his youngest daughter wanted. At last he climbed into his carriage and set off for home.

While he rode, he thought about his daughters. As for the horses, they took the short way to the palace. Suddenly the carriage stopped.

The padişah looked up in surprise. There was the carriage, mired in the mud. The padişah touched the horses' backs with the whip. They pulled and pulled, but they could not move the carriage at all.

The padişah sent his footman to get more horses, but even pulling all together, they could not move the carriage out of the mud.

"*Now* what am I to do?" sighed the padişah.

Suddenly, "*Grmph, grmph, grmph*," there was an ugly old pig rooting through the mud. The padişah pulled his arms back inside the carriage. Ugh! What a filthy creature!

"*Grmph, grmph, grmph*," said the pig. "I can push you out of the mud."

"Well, then," said the padişah, "*push*."

"*Grmph, grmph, grmph*," grunted the pig. "First you must promise to give me your youngest daughter as my bride."

The padişah swallowed hard. Give his favorite daughter to a *pig*? Never! On the other hand, he could not just stay there in the mud . . .

"Very well," he said, "you may have my youngest daughter. Quickly, now! Push my carriage out of the mud."

"*Grmph, grmph, grmph!*" grunted the pig. And with one push of his snout, the carriage was out of the mud and onto the road. Off drove the padişah, without even a thank-you for the pig, ugly old thing that he was.

The oldest daughter was glad for her golden gown. The second daughter swished here and there in her silver sash. And the youngest was so sweet-tempered that she didn't mind the least bit that her father hadn't brought her

> Grapes that speak,
> Apples that smile,
> And apricots that tinkle in the breeze.

As for his promise to the pig, the padişah never said a word about it. After all, what use would a *pig* have for a princess!

Still, late that afternoon there was a *"Grmph, grmph, grmph"* in the palace courtyard. The padişah rushed to the door, and, sure enough, there was that ugly old pig, hauling a wheelbarrow. *"Grmph, grmph, grmph.* I have come for your daughter," said the pig.

"Oh, dear!" thought the padişah. And he called a maid from the kitchen. She was quickly dressed in a fine silk gown, with slippers to match. "Here you are," said the padişah as he set the girl carefully in the wheelbarrow.

"Grmph, grmph, grmph," grunted the pig crossly, and he tipped the girl out of the wheelbarrow into the dust. "I came for your youngest daughter," said he, "and it is your youngest daughter that I want."

Well, there was nothing to do but to tell his youngest daughter all about it. Nonetheless, he had her dressed in a ragged gown, with torn slippers. Perhaps the pig would not want her, after all.

But the pig knew a beautiful, sweet-tempered girl when he saw one. *"Grmph, grmph, grmph,"* he grunted happily. "Yes, this is the one I want." And he tucked her into the wheelbarrow and trundled her off down the road.

"There goes my daughter," sighed the padişah. "And all for being stuck fast in the mud!"

The pig and the princess went along and went along and went along till they came to a tumbledown old pigsty. *"Grmph, grmph, grmph.* Here is your new home," said the pig, and he helped her down from the wheelbarrow. Into the pigsty they went.

"Grmph, grmph, grmph," said the pig, pointing with his trotter to the trough. "You'll find corn a-plenty to eat. And over there"—he pointed to straw littering one corner—"that is your bed."

Now, the princess was a good-tempered girl, and this wasn't exactly what she was used to. Still, she munched away at the corn, and early in the evening she curled herself up to sleep in the straw. But once the pig was snoring away, the princess wept salt tears for sorrow. At last, she too fell asleep.

The sun was high in the sky by the time she awoke. And what was this! She found herself lying in a feather bed, with sheets of softest silk. The bedroom in which she lay was finer than her own room in the palace. And everywhere there were maids to wait upon her.

She rubbed her eyes in astonishment, and when she looked again, there stood a smiling young man, handsome as the full moon. "You see, my dear," said he, "this is my palace, and you are my queen. As soon as I came to the throne, a wicked enchantment was worked upon me, and I was turned into an ugly pig. Only one thing would release me from the spell: I must be able to win a girl who asked for

> Grapes that speak,
> Apples that smile,
> And apricots that tinkle in the breeze.

Come, now, to the garden and see for yourself." And he led her down a winding staircase to the garden.

"Good morning, my queen," said the grapes, thick upon the vine. Apples smiled at her from every bough. And, true enough, golden apricots tinkled as the breeze touched them.

The princess sighed happily. "Let us go this very day and tell my father," she said.

The young king and the princess went in a fine coach to the padişah's palace. He was overjoyed to hear the news. A splendid wedding was celebrated for forty days and forty nights. As for the young king and his bride, they had all their wishes fulfilled. May we have a share of their good fortune!

The Princess and the Goatherd

Once there was and once there wasn't, in times long gone, when Allah's creatures were plentiful and to talk too much was a sin—well, in those times there was a padişah who decided of a sudden to travel in disguise throughout his kingdom. Calling his servants, he had himself dressed as a merchant, and then he set off.

He walked and walked, seeing little that was surprising, and nothing that was truly new. As he was turning home toward his palace, well satisfied with affairs in his broad land, he saw in the distance an old, old man. The old man sat at the edge of a stream, and as he sat, he cut away at something in his hands.

Wondering, the padişah drew nearer to the old man. Scarcely moving, the white-bearded old fellow snipped away with his scissors, and then he dropped whatever he had cut into the stream, and watched as it was carried away by the water.

"Father," said the padişah, "I am curious. What is it that you are doing?"

"I am cutting the fortunes of men, and I am throwing them into this stream, which carries them into the river of life," replied the old man, still intent upon what he was doing.

The padişah thought about this strange answer. Then, earnest to know what fate held in store for his beloved daughter, he made bold to ask. "Eh!" said he, "look a little, if you will, into the future of my only child. Tell me, what do you see there?"

"I have just this moment cut your daughter's fortune and sent it forth upon the stream," said the old man, seeing past the merchant's robe into the heart of the padişah.

"And what *is* it?" asked the padişah eagerly.

In answer, the old man pointed to a field on the steep hillside. "Do you see that field? Well, the fate of your daughter lies with the young goatherd who pastures his flock in that field." Saying no more, the old man returned to his work.

His only daughter to be the bride of a goatherd! Such a fate must never befall one so beautiful as she . . . That matter decided, the padişah bent his steps toward the faraway field. At last, just before coming upon the young goatherd, the padişah formed a plan.

"Good afternoon, my son," he said. "I have long desired a fine flock of goats, but never have I seen likelier animals than yours. What should you say to selling them?"

To his surprise, the young goatherd chose not to sell his flock at all.

"But," pursued the padişah, "what if I were to offer you a thousand pieces of gold?"

Still the goatherd shook his head. "Sire," he answered, "even a thousand pieces of gold could not buy the worth of my fine goats."

Concealing his annoyance, the padişah continued, "And if a thousand pieces of gold will not buy them, what would you say to a whole chest of gold pieces?"

The young goatherd considered the matter this way and that. Then, "But, sire, where is the chest?" he asked.

"Ah," said the padişah, "you will have to go to the padişah's palace for it. But"—as the goatherd looked surprised—"you will have no difficulty, for I myself am the padişah, and I shall give you a letter to carry to my vizier. He will provide you with what you deserve."

"But my goats—" began the young man.

"I shall stay here and tend your goats myself. After all, they will soon be *my* goats, and who would take better care of them than I?" He prepared the letter for the goatherd, a simple note that read, "Kill the bearer of this letter, and be sure that this has been accomplished before my return."

The goatherd, unable to read the letter but certain of its importance, put it carefully in a little leather bag on a thong around his neck. Then he hurried off toward the palace. Up hill and down dale he went, on a journey greater than any he had traveled before, but at length he came in sight of the palace.

The towers of the palace stood so tall and grand, and he felt so small and tired, that the young goatherd decided he would do well to rest before he approached the vizier with the padişah's message. Choosing a shady spot near the public fountain directly across the road from the palace, the young man lay down and in three or five minutes was sound asleep.

Meanwhile, the princess, for want of something more interesting to do, had been looking down on the street from her window. Seeing the young man, she felt somehow drawn to him. A stranger he was, but young and handsome. And what was that which he carried so carefully around his neck? Calling a servant, the princess said, "Go at once to the olive tree nearest the public fountain. There you will find a young man asleep with a leather bag around his neck. Remove the bag very carefully, so as not to awaken the young man, and bring the bag to me."

Hastening to do the princess's bidding, the servant was back in good time with the bag. On reading the letter, the princess was moved with pity, and she resolved that the young man should not die. Quickly she wrote another letter: "Wash and purify the bearer of this letter and marry him at once to my daughter. Be sure that this has been accomplished before my return." Then she sealed the letter with the royal seal and, placing it in the little leather bag, she had the servant return the bag to the neck of the sleeping goatherd.

The goatherd, awaking at last, carried the letter to the vizier. Imagine the astonishment of the vizier on reading the message! But what could he do? One dared not question an order from the padişah. And everything was therefore speedily accomplished as had been directed in the letter.

Just as the flutes and the drums had begun to play, celebrating the wedding of the princess, the padişah arrived. The goats could take care of themselves; he must be sure that the vizier had taken proper care of the young goatherd.

"What is this?" he asked a passing peasant. "For whose wedding are the flutes and the drums being played?"

"Oh, haven't you heard the news? It is the wedding of the

padişah's only daughter," the peasant replied. "I have not seen the man, but it is said that he is young and handsome."

A-tremble with rage, the padişah went at once to question his vizier. The vizier, reaching into the folds of his sash, brought forth the letter. "Here, sire, are the words which set those flutes to playing."

It took but a moment for the padişah to see in the changed message both the hand of his daughter and the prediction of the old man. He became even more determined to put an end to this unwanted son-in-law. But how? If the young man had been kept unaware of the deception, he would be willing to carry another letter . . .

Summoning his daughter's husband, the padişah greeted him quite as if he had planned the wedding all himself. And this young man so recently a goatherd fell readily into the trap prepared for him. "Come, my son," said the padişah gravely. "You have performed so handsomely on your first errand that I have another letter to entrust to you." In the young man's hands was placed a letter to the candlemaker, addressed in a flowing Arabic script and richly decorated with the royal seal. Within the packet was nothing, no message at all, though the padişah took care to tell him how important the contents were. "Tomorrow morning before dawn, my son, you must deliver this directly to the candlemaker. This is perhaps the most important order ever delivered for the safety of the kingdom, and you above all should be most deeply concerned with it."

Kissing the padişah's hand and raising it to his own forehead, the young man promised that dawn would find him at the candlemaker's. Once the trusting young fellow had returned to his bride, the padişah summoned his vizier. "Since letters can be tampered with, you are to carry this most important message from mouth to ear," he directed. "Go at once to the candlemaker. Tell him that just before dawn tomorrow a traitor to the throne will appear, a man determined to take the fate of this whole kingdom into his own hands. As soon as this traitor crosses the threshold, the candlemaker—without even looking to identify the man or to listen to his protests—is to throw him alive into the boiler. Remember, he is to act at the very *moment* the man

enters the door." At once, the vizier left to carry out the padişah's order.

Well before dawn the next morning, the young man arose
and dressed. With special care he placed the padişah's message
in the little leather bag around his neck. Just as he was slipping
past the princess's bed, the bride awoke. In truth, the two already loved each other very much, and the princess was reluc-
tant to spend even an hour apart from her sweetheart. By one
means and another, she persuaded him to tell her of his errand,
and she, no fool at all, feared the outcome of his visit to the
candlemaker. Without a hint of her worry for his safety, she
managed to keep him with her until the sun had appeared at
the edge of the minaret. The young man, noticing the sun, bade
her a hasty goodbye, and set off for the candlemaker's.

But, as Allah would have it, someone had gone before him.
For the padişah, unable to conceal his impatience to learn if his
order had indeed been carried out, had hurried to the candlemaker's just before the first streak of dawn had touched the sky.
At the very moment the door had opened, he had been seized
by the candlemaker and thrown alive into the boiler. As the
padişah himself had said so often when disposing of a threat to
his throne, "He who digs a pit for his neighbor should dig it his
own size." And there is much truth in that saying.

As for the goatherd, he ascended to the throne as the husband of the dead padişah's daughter, and the two lived happily
for many years. May we have a share of their happiness.

Hamal Hasan and the Baby Day

Hasan looked around the busy market. His big basket hung empty on his back. "Hamal! Hamal! Hamal!" he called out. "Let me carry your bundles!" It was Hamal Hasan shouting.

A stout woman hurried up to him. On one arm she carried a sleeping baby. Packages of all kinds were in her other hand. "Hamal!" she said. "How much will you charge to take my baby and my packages to Süleyman Mosque?"

Now, Hasan was newly arrived in İstanbul, so he had no idea where to find Süleyman Mosque. He did want to earn some money, though, to buy his bread and cheese. "You can pay me whatever you wish," he said politely. He stood still while she dropped her packages into his basket. Carefully he took the sleeping baby in his arms. "Now," said the stout woman, "follow me." And off she set with quick steps toward the market gate.

Hasan hurried after her, being careful not to bump the baby. Just as they came to the street, Hasan saw a man from his village. At last he could have some news of his family!

"Good morning, neighbor," he said. And his friend happily stopped to talk with him. They chatted, forgetting about everything else in the noisy market. At last Hasan was satisfied that he had heard all the village news. "Goodbye, neighbor," he said. "May your way be open." And he looked for the woman he was to follow.

Where *was* she? He looked everywhere, tugging at the sleeve of every stout woman he saw. She was nowhere to be found! Hasan scratched his head. What was he to do?

"How do I go to Süleyman Mosque?" he asked a shopkeeper.

"Go out that gate," said the shopkeeper, "and just follow your nose. You can't miss it."

Hasan set off at a half-trot toward the gate. He joggled the baby, and the baby awoke. "*Wah!* *Wah!*" the baby cried.

"*Sh*, baby! *Sh*, baby!" said Hasan.

The baby cried even harder when it heard Hasan's strange voice. Hasan rocked the baby and even *sang* to it. Still, the baby cried.

Trying not to listen, Hasan hurried down the street. He could see the mosque far ahead of him. Finally he reached the fountain in the mosque courtyard. Where was the woman? She was nowhere in sight. Hasan waited and waited. He asked everyone, "Have you seen the mother of this child?" No one had time to help him.

Finally Hasan asked a ragged beggar who sat on a stone near the fountain. He told the beggar the whole story. "Listen carefully," said the beggar. "I will tell you what to do. Do you see the platform where the funeral coffin is kept?"

"Yes," Hasan nodded.

"Yesterday I saw a woman put a baby on that platform. The baby stayed there for an hour or two. Then the baby's mother came and took him away. You should do the same thing with this baby. Don't worry. His mother will soon find him."

"That is a fine idea," said Hasan. And, walking quickly to the platform, Hasan put the baby there. He was afraid to leave the baby alone, so he hid and watched.

Suddenly he felt someone beating him on the back. It was an angry old woman. "So *you* are the one who puts babies on the platform!" she shouted, beating him with her fists. "You wait right here. I'll be back in a minute!" And she hurried to her home across the street. Back she came with *another* baby. "Here," she said, thrusting the baby into Hasan's arms. "You wicked man! Here is the one you left yesterday. The *next* time you put a poor innocent baby out to cry, I shall call the police. Now go get that other poor baby and be off with you!" And she watched while Hasan picked up the first baby from the platform.

"Well," thought Hasan sadly. "Here I am with *two* babies. What shall I do?"

Finally he started back toward the market.

Hasan stood just outside the public bath. Another porter came by, on his way to market for a new load of parcels. "Well, brother, you have two babies! Why do you look so distressed?"

Hasan told him the whole sad story, and the crying babies added their own shrill chorus. "What shall I do?" he asked.

"That's easy," said the other porter. "You see that public bath over there? Take the babies there and tell the woman in charge that their mother will come for them in a few minutes."

Hasan hurried to the bath. He knocked on the door and waited anxiously for the bath attendant. When she came, he said, "Madam, I was told to leave these babies here for their mother to pick up."

"Oh, you were, were you?" said the bath attendant. "Just wait here a minute." She hurried into the bathhouse. Back she came with *another* baby. "You wicked man!" she scolded. "You came here with a baby yesterday. Take the poor little thing back wherever he belongs. And don't bring me any more babies!"

"But, madam, what am I to do with this one? I already have two babies that don't belong to me!"

"That is your worry, not mine," said the woman. She put the third baby in the basket, and then she slammed the door. The babies began to cry.

"What am I to do now?" groaned Hasan. He stood, discouraged, in the crowded street.

Meanwhile, what had become of the stout woman? She had hurried along to the mosque, thinking Hasan was following her. When she came to the mosque, she turned to get her baby and her packages. But her baby was gone, and so was the porter. She began to weep and to tear her hair in grief. Then, thinking that he might have gone back to the market, she hurried there. But Hasan was nowhere to be found. Finally she saw one of the sultan's guards. "My baby has been stolen!" she cried. "Please help me!"

The guard listened to her story. Then he called four other guards. "A thieving porter has stolen this woman's baby," he said. "Spread out through the city and look for a porter carrying a baby." And they all hurried away to look.

The biggest, burliest one happened to find Hasan. "Three babies!" he cried. "What a thief! Come with me at once!" He led Hasan to Süleyman Mosque. All three babies began to howl at once, and everyone stopped to stare. At last they saw the stout woman.

"Oh, my blessed baby!" She snatched her baby from Hasan. "Poor baby! I thought I would never see you again!" After hearing Hasan's tale of woe, she handed him a silver coin.

Hasan then told the guards the whole story. They all burst into laughter, slapping their knees with delight. Then the captain of the guards said, "We must report this to the sultan." And he led Hasan before the sultan himself.

Once more, Hasan told the whole story. "Ho, ho, ho!" laughed the sultan. "That's the funniest story I have heard in a long time."

"But, sire, what shall I do with these other two babies?" asked Hasan.

"We'll keep the babies in the guardhouse and send out a notice that they have been found. Their mothers will soon come for them, as they always do. Meanwhile, here are some coins for your trouble." And the sultan gave Hasan a handful of shiny coins.

As for Hasan, he thanked the sultan over and over, partly for the silver coins, but mostly for taking the babies. Then he hurried out into the street.

"Never again will I carry a baby, even for a *hundred* silver coins," he said. And as far as we know, he never did.

The Round Sultan
and the Straight Answer

Once there was and twice there wasn't a Turkish sultan who loved to eat. Three or five times a day he sat himself down at his dining tray. One after another he ate *yoğurt* soup and rice with yoğurt and meats with yoğurt and fruits with yoğurt. Great heaps of dark brown bread simply melted away.

All around the sultan sat his courtiers, nibbling away at this and that. Musicians played. Beautiful veiled girls danced. A fountain splashed, and multicolored birds sang in their cages. Altogether, mealtimes were splendid times indeed.

Each day, the sultan was weighed in his royal set of scales. The sultan smiled to see that he was growing at last to be a fine figure of a ruler. He must surely be the fattest sultan in all the world, he thought.

But every good has its bad. One day the scales broke beneath his weight.

That day, too, the sultan discovered that he was too fat to walk a single step. His feet hurt hideously if he stood up even for a moment. His royal throne developed a crack which widened and widened. Finally the royal carpenters had to make another throne, twice as strong and sturdy as the first one.

One by one, the sultan's royal shirts and royal trousers split at the seams. Tailors were called to make new clothes.

The sultan could no longer fit into the royal bathtub. A new one was made, large enough to bathe two full-grown buffaloes. Ten men helped the sultan into his bath. Ten men helped him out again.

Clearly, the sultan had become too fat. Something must be done before matters became any worse. Criers went out to the ends of the kingdom. "The sultan seeks a doctor. Who can help the sultan become thinner? Hear ye! Hear ye! Your reward will be great!"

Doctors hurried to the palace from all directions. Some brought books of healing. Some brought medicines. All of them were certain they could help the sultan.

The first doctor studied the sultan. Then he said solemnly, "My sultan, you must eat nothing but fruit."

The sultan tried for seven days to eat nothing but fruit. He had fruit for breakfast, fruit for lunch, fruit for afternoon tea, and fruit for dinner. He *tried* to eat nothing but fruit. Oh, he ate between meals, now and then—a heap of rice with chicken made a pleasant snack. And nothing tasted better than a tray of honeyed baklava. At the end of a week, the first doctor came to examine the sultan. Alas, the sultan was fatter than ever. "To prison with him!" roared the sultan. "Give him nothing but fruit. As for me, fruit simply won't do."

A second doctor studied the sultan. Then he said solemnly, "My sultan, you must take nothing but hot tea without sugar."

The sultan tried for seven days to take nothing but hot tea without sugar. He had hot tea without sugar for breakfast, hot tea without sugar for lunch, hot tea without sugar for afternoon tea, and hot tea without sugar for dinner. Oh, he ate between meals now and then, because he was so hungry. A heap of rice with chicken made a tasty snack. And he *did* relish honeyed baklava. At the end of a week, the second doctor came to examine the sultan. Alas, the sultan was fatter than ever. "To prison with him!" roared the sultan. "Give him nothing but hot tea without sugar. As for me, hot tea without sugar simply won't do."

More doctors came. "Give the sultan steam baths every day," said one. The sultan steamed and steamed. Between steam baths he ate and ate. And off to prison went another doctor.

"Exercise!"

"Nothing but meat!"

"Smaller helpings!"

"No music and dancing at meals!"

"No company at meals!"

"Less sleep!"

"Nothing but yoğurt!"

"Massage him and pummel him four times a day!"

"Give him these special pills!"

One after another, forty doctors tried their remedies. One after another, off to prison they went, each one condemned to his own remedy. As for the sultan, he grew fatter and fatter.

Then one day a clever hamal chanced to pass the palace. On his back he carried the furniture of a whole house. "Hamal!" called the sultan's vizier. "You are needed in the palace."

The hamal set down his burden. He hurried after the vizier. At last they arrived before the sultan. "You can carry the furniture from a whole house," said the vizier. "Lift our sultan into his bed."

For a moment the hamal studied the sultan. He had heard about the sultan's problem—*everybody* had heard about the sultan's problem. The hamal said boldly, "What does it matter whether he sits on his throne or lies in his bed? He will be dead in another forty days anyway!"

The sultan gasped. "How dare you!" he shouted. Then, in a voice scarcely louder than a whisper, he asked, "How do you know?"

"I just *know*," answered the hamal. "Believe me. You will be dead in forty days."

"He lies! Take him off to prison," ordered the sultan. And two servants dragged the hamal down the winding stone steps to the dungeon.

As for the sultan, suddenly he had lost his appetite. Only forty days more to live! He gnawed at his lips. He bit his fingernails. He groaned and sighed.

At breakfast he nibbled at toast.

At lunch he had a bit of white cheese.

At afternoon tea he sampled a plum cake.

At dinner he forced down a small *kebab.*

As for eating between meals, somehow food didn't seem important anymore.

Day after day passed. The sultan sat and worried. At the end of the twentieth day he arose. His feet felt numb, but he could walk again. He paced the floor hour after hour. Only twenty days more to live!

His royal shirts and his royal trousers sagged and bagged. Something strange had happened to them. They were *much* too big.

At the end of the thirty-ninth day, the sultan called his vizier. "Tomorrow I shall die," he said. "You must write out my last will and testament." He sighed as he passed the kingdom on to his younger brother. Who would have thought that the fattest sultan in the world would have ended in such a way?

The fortieth day came and went. All day the sultan paced the floor, from the east windows to the west windows, from the north windows to the south windows. He sighed as he gazed out at the rows of houses below. What a pity to leave such a fine kingdom! But tonight was to be his last.

The forty-first day dawned sunny and bright. From the minaret came the familiar call to prayer. Birds sang in the trees of the sultan's garden. The sultan awoke.

He rubbed his eyes sleepily. Then suddenly he sat up. This was the forty-first day! He was still alive. "Praise be to Allah!" he rejoiced. "Send for that hamal!"

The vizier himself hurried down the stone steps to the dungeon. Forty doctors, all of them thin as thin, bowed as the vizier entered. The hamal arose. "Sire," he said, "this is the forty-first day."

"You are right," agreed the vizier. "The sultan has sent for you."

The hamal followed the vizier up the winding steps. What would happen now? What could he say to the sultan?

"There you are!" exclaimed the sultan, propping himself up in bed. "You said I was to die in forty days. This is the forty-first day. You lied!"

"That may be," answered the hamal. Then his eyes twinkled. "But see, sire. You are thin!"

For a moment the sultan was speechless. Then a great smile spread across his face. He leaped out of bed. He waltzed about the room in his flapping royal pajamas. He felt his thin arms, his thin legs, his thin neck. Yes, he *was* thin.

"Bring me a new pair of scales!" he shouted.

The servants hurried in with the stoutest pair of scales in the kingdom. The sultan stepped into the dish at one side of the scales. "Now fill up the other dish with gold until the scales exactly balance," he ordered.

And the servants piled gold by the handful into the dish until the great heap exactly balanced the smiling sultan. "This gold, hamal, is your reward for your great wisdom," declared the sultan. "Take it, and may your way be open."

The hamal gathered up his treasure and with a thankful heart left the palace. One by one, the forty doctors climbed the stone steps and went about their business.

As for the sultan, he became no fatter than a sensible sultan should be. And as far as I know, he is ruling yet.

A Mirror, a Carpet, and a Lemon

Once there was and once there wasn't a sultan who had a beautiful daughter named Perihan. Princes from all over the world heard about her beauty. They came, one after another, seeking to marry her.

"The prince who will marry my daughter must bring me the most wonderful gift in the world," said the sultan.

"And what is that?" asked one of the princes.

"You will have to find out for yourself," answered the sultan.

One after another the princes came back with unusual gifts for the sultan. One brought a bird that could sing without stopping. Another brought an ivory fountain that would never stop flowing. A third brought a sheep with fleece of gold. But the sultan shook his head. "These are fine gifts," he said, "but they are not exactly what I had in mind."

"He doesn't really know what he wants," one prince muttered. And they all went away, discouraged.

Now, far, far away there were three princes who were brothers. "Let us go to seek the princess Perihan in marriage," said one.

"Yes," agreed the second.

"And I shall go, too," said the third.

The other two laughed, but they let him come, anyway.

Each one of the princes had five thousand pieces of gold to spend on a gift for the sultan. The first prince bought a mirror that was very special. By looking into the mirror, he could see what was going on anywhere in the world. "I am sure the sultan will like my gift the best," he said.

The second prince bought a carpet with his five thousand pieces of gold. But it was a very special carpet. He could sit on the carpet and travel anywhere in the world that he wished to go. All he had to do was to name the place, and the carpet would take him there.

The third prince looked and looked, but he could not find anything that pleased him. Finally, just before his brothers were ready to leave him behind, he went once more to the bazaar. A new merchant was there. "Lemons! Lemons!" he called. And the prince was curious.

"Tell me about your lemons," he said.

"These are magic lemons. The juice from them will heal any illness in the world."

"How much is one lemon?" asked the prince.

"Five thousand pieces of gold," the merchant said.

The prince thought and thought. "Perhaps this gift would please the sultan." So he paid all his five thousand pieces of gold for one lemon.

The next day, the three princes set out for the sultan's country. That first night, they stopped at an inn. They began to talk about the princess Perihan.

"I shall marry the princess," declared the first prince. "The sultan will think my mirror is the most unusual gift of all."

"No, indeed," said the second prince. "He will like my magic carpet best."

"And what of my lemon?" asked the third prince.

His brothers just laughed. "Who but a fool would pay five thousand pieces of gold for a *lemon*?" jeered the first prince.

"Never mind," said the second prince. "You can be there to see me marry the princess Perihan."

"I wonder how she is?" asked the youngest prince.

"I'll look in my mirror and see," said the first prince. He looked in his mirror, and, behold! The princess Perihan lay very ill in the sultan's palace.

"We must hurry," said the second prince. "Get on my carpet, and we shall go there at once."

So the three princes got on the carpet, and in less time than it takes to say so, they were at the sultan's palace.

The sultan was weeping. He scarcely saw the three princes. "My poor Perihan!" he cried.

"My sultan," said the youngest prince, "I have here a lemon that may help your daughter."

"A *lemon!*"

"Yes, my sultan. The juice from this lemon can cure any illness in the world." So the youngest prince squeezed the lemon and gave the juice to the princess Perihan.

In a few moments, the color returned to her face. She sat up, smiling. She was well!

The sultan turned to the princes. "Now, what was it that you wanted?" he asked.

"We came to marry the princess," said the first prince. "I have brought you a magic mirror. Only see! You can look into it and see whatever is going on anywhere in the world."

"You are right. It is a wonderful mirror," agreed the sultan.

"Yes. It was by looking into this mirror that we discovered the princess was ill. I think *I* ought to have the princess in marriage."

"But it was my carpet that brought us here in time!" said the second prince. "Here, my sultan. It will take you anywhere you wish to go. I think *I* ought to marry the princess."

"It is an unusual carpet, and very useful," agreed the sultan. "But you, youngest prince, what have you brought?"

"I brought the lemon," said the youngest prince, "and here it is." And he gave to the sultan the squeezed-out lemon.

His brothers just laughed. But the princess Perihan did not laugh. "Father," she said, "have you decided which was the most unusual gift of all?"

"Both the mirror and the carpet are most unusual," he said.

"But the lemon was the greatest gift, after all, my father. It gave me back my life, and life is surely the greatest gift of all," said the princess.

"You are right, my daughter," said the sultan. "He could use the lemon only once, but with it he saved your life. He deserves to marry you."

Thus it was that the youngest prince wed Perihan, in a wedding that lasted forty days and forty nights. They had their wish fulfilled. May we be as fortunate as they!

New Patches for Old

One day, Hasan the shoemaker closed his shop a bit early. "Tomorrow evening the holidays begin," he said. "I'll buy something new for my family."

For his wife he bought a blouse. For his mother he bought a scarf. And for his married daughter he bought four bright hair ribbons.

Then, looking down at his own clothes, he said, "I *must* buy a new pair of trousers for myself. These old ones are just patches on patches."

He hurried to the tailor's shop. "Have you trousers to fit me?" he asked.

"See for yourself," said the tailor. "I have only one pair left."

Hasan held that pair up against his old ones. "They seem all right around the waist," he said, "but they're three fingers too long. Can you shorten them?"

"Not today," said the tailor. "Ask your wife to shorten them."

"All right," said Hasan. He paid the tailor and hastened home with his parcels.

His wife liked her blouse. "How fine!" she said. "And what did *you* get?"

"I bought these trousers," Hasan answered, "but they're three fingers too long. Could you shorten them?"

"Not now," she said. "I want to sew sequins on my new blouse. Why not ask your mother? She does everything so well!"

"All right," said Hasan, and along he went to his mother's house.

"Mother," he said, "I've bought you a new scarf for the holidays."

"How fine!" she said. "And what did you buy for yourself?"

"These trousers," he answered, "but they're three fingers too long. Could you shorten them?"

"Son, I have no time for sewing. The holidays begin tomorrow, and I must pray for our dead relatives. Why not ask your daughter? She should be good for *something*."

"All right," Hasan said, and along he went to his daughter's house.

"Daughter," he said, "I've bought you some ribbons for the holidays."

"How fine!" said his daughter. "And what did you buy for yourself?"

"These trousers," he answered, "but they're three fingers too long. Could you shorten them?"

"Oh, no, Father!" she said. "I must feed the baby, and then I'll iron my ribbons. Surely *my* mother or *your* mother will shorten them."

Hasan thought and thought. Then he hurried to his shop. Carefully he cut a piece three fingers wide from the end of each trouser leg. With his big shoemaker's needle he put new hems in the trousers. Then, folding them over his arm, he went along home and put them on his shelf.

The next afternoon, Hasan closed his shop very early. Nodding to this one and smiling at that one, he strolled home. Everyone was feeling the happiness of the holidays.

His wife met him at the door. "Come in," she said. "Your mother and our daughter are here."

Hasan was surprised. His mother? His daughter?

Hasan's mother looked lovely in her new scarf. "As soon as you're ready, Son, we'll all go to the festival together," she said. Then she smiled to herself, for she had a fine secret.

"Husband, *do* be quick," said his wife. "Put on those new trousers. See? I am wearing my new blouse." She was smiling to herself, for she had a fine secret.

And, "Please, Father, don't be long," urged his daughter, with her new ribbons blooming in her hair. She, too, was smiling about a secret of her own.

136

Ah, they are all fine-looking women, thought Hasan, even if they hadn't had the time to do his sewing. He would be pleased to take them with him to the festival.

And he went into the bedroom to put on his new trousers, trousers exactly right around the waist *and* exactly the right length. He ought to know, for hadn't he shortened them himself?

Suddenly, *"Eyvah!"* cried Hasan.

"Are you sick?" called his wife.

"No—oh, no. But *something* has happened to my trousers!" And, opening the door, he stood there to show them what he meant. His fine new trousers hung just below his knees.

Hasan's wife and Hasan's mother and Hasan's daughter all said, "But I shortened them only three fingers!" Then, realizing what must have happened, they stared at Hasan.

As for Hasan, he stared back at them, too stunned to speak.

"My dear," said his wife, "last night while you were out visiting your friends, I remembered the trousers. 'He's such a good husband,' I said to myself. 'I'll shorten his trousers while he's gone.'

"There was *such* a clumsy hem at the bottom of each leg! But I ripped out the hems and cut exactly three fingers off the ends. Then I hemmed them neatly and put them back on your shelf."

Hasan's mother smiled ruefully. "I came this morning after your wife had gone to do her marketing. I had finished my prayers, and I said to myself, 'Hasan is such a good son. I'll shorten his trousers now.' I found the trousers and let down the hems and cut a piece exactly three fingers' width from the ends of the legs. I made neat hems in them and folded them and put them on your shelf. I wanted to surprise you!"

"Oh, you *did*, Mother!" Hasan said, smiling despite himself.

Then it was his daughter's turn. "Father, I was rocking my baby this morning when I remembered your trousers. 'He's such a kind father,' I said to myself. 'I *must* shorten his trousers.' So I bundled up the baby and hurried over here.

"I found the trousers and took out the hems and trimmed three fingers' width from each leg and put in new hems. Then

I folded the trousers and put them back on your shelf and took the baby along home. I wanted it to be a nice surprise for you."

Hasan looked from one to the other. Then he laughed. "But *I* had already shortened them myself!"

"*You?*" they exclaimed.

"Yes. *Someone* had to do it, so I cut off the ends and hemmed them up myself."

Suddenly they all shouted with laughter. And, in the middle of their laughing, they thought what they could do: they could sew most of the pieces back onto the trousers. As Allah would have it, when they had finished, the trousers were exactly the right length.

"Well, my dears," said Hasan, "at least all my patches are *new* patches!"

And, dressed in their holiday finery, away they went to the festival.

Hasan and Allah's Greatness

Once there was and once there wasn't a padişah who was a very, very proud man, and he had just one daughter. One day he called his daughter and said, "Tell me. Who is richer than we are?"

His daughter answered, "Allah is, my father."

"Oh, no, my daughter," said he. And he was angry.

He asked again, another day, "Daughter, tell me. Who is richer than we are?"

She repeated, "Allah. Of course, Allah is, Father."

"Oh, no, indeed!" said her father. And he was very angry.

And he asked a third time, "Daughter, tell me. Who is richer than we are?"

The third time she answered the same way. "It's Allah, Father." And she wouldn't change her mind.

Just then the padişah looked through the window and saw a *simit* seller passing by. He said to a servant, "Go and call that man, and tell him to come here."

So the servant stopped the simit seller and said, "Come in right away. The padişah wants you."

Well, the simit seller began to weep. "But I haven't done anything wrong," he said. "Please don't take me there."

The servant said, "Whether you have done wrong or right, you are asked by the padişah to go to his side, and you had better come in."

He left his wooden simit tray by the side of the stairs and *patur kitur patur kitur* went upstairs to the padişah. "Here I am, Your Majesty," he said. "What do you desire?"

And the padişah said, "This is what I want of you. I'm going to marry my daughter to you, right away, right here, today, and you'll take her away."

The poor man said, "Oh, Your Majesty, how can that be? How can I take your daughter as my wife? I have no place to live, and I have nothing to eat. I have no family. I am just a poor simit seller."

But the padişah answered. "I am *ordering* you so, and you have to obey, or else your head will be cut off! Go down now," he said, "and find a hoca and bring him here to perform your marriage ceremony. Then hold my daughter's hand and go away wherever you will."

The simit seller went down, and out into the street. Poor thing, he was just a young fellow, and nothing like that had ever happened to him before. He looked here and there, and finally he saw a hoca passing by. "Oh, please, sir, come on," he said. "I have some business for you to perform."

The hoca came and married the young man to the padişah's daughter. And just as the padişah had ordered, he held her hand and they started on their way, with the wooden simit tray on his head and the girl on his arm. They started going, but he didn't know where he should take her.

There was an innkeeper he knew, and he went to that inn and said, "Oh, please, friend, I have a wife and I have no place to stay. Please give me a room here. I'll see to it that I'll pay you for it by and by."

They went into the room. It was bare as could be. There was only a straw mat on the floor. There wasn't even a glass to drink a drop of water. He put the girl in the room and locked the door on her and went out to sell his simits. He worked very, very hard trying to sell all his simits. And then he bought a loaf of bread, some olives, and a little cheese, and came home to eat.

It happened this way every day. If he had enough money to add something to the loaf of bread, he did. If he did not have enough money, they just sat down and ate bread, and they never complained.

Finally the husband saw that there was no good to come from selling simits. This wouldn't be enough to make life possible for them. So one day he said to his wife, "Let me stop selling simits and become a porter, a hamal. Maybe I shall be able to earn more money." So he did. He left his simit tray and he started carrying things for people. He went here and there, and carried loads and luggage and bundles for people, and he made a little bit more money, so he was able to buy a mattress for them and to buy a rug for the floor and a little kettle to boil water or to cook things in—plain and simple things—a pitcher, and two glasses to drink out of, and a little better food to eat. And all the time he was giving some money to the innkeeper, too, saying, "Please excuse me for not being able to pay you regularly." The innkeeper was a good man, and he always answered, "It doesn't matter. You're my brother and she's my sister."

Now there were some traveling merchants on their way to Baghdad to buy things and bring them back. But they needed a very strong man to carry their loads. While they were looking for a man to carry for them, the innkeeper said, "Why don't you take Hamal Hasan? He's a mighty man—he's a strong and mighty man—and he's a good man. You take Hamal Hasan along with you."

Then the innkeeper called Hasan and said, "Here is a good job for you. You'll go to Baghdad with these merchants and you'll earn much money."

Hamal Hasan said, "All right. It's good, as you say, but you know how it is with me. I have my wife and I earn my bread daily. If I leave her and go away, she won't have anything to eat. If they'd give me some money in advance, I could leave it with her so she could have enough to eat while I am gone."

The innkeeper said, "Don't worry about that. She's my sister, and I'll take good care of her."

But the merchants gave Hasan some money to leave for his wife, and then they took Hamal Hasan along with them on their way. They went and they went. They went a little; they went far. They went straight over rivers and over dales. They went six months and a summer, until they found themselves in a desert. It was hot—oh, it was hot! There was no water, and there was no rest.

When they were very desperate, they came across a well in the desert at the bottom of which there was water. The chief merchant said, "Let's tie a rope around the waist of one of the hamals and let him down into the well to bring some water out for us." So they did this, saying, "You bring some water for us to drink, and to fill the barrels, and to water the animals, because they'll perish without water."

The man said, "All right." But when he was part of the way down into the well he began screaming, "Oh, I'm burning! I'm burning! Oh, I'm burning!" So they pulled him out.

Another hamal said, "Let me. I can do it." They tied a rope around his waist and they let him down into the well. But when he was part of the way down, he started screaming, "I'm freezing! I'm freezing! It's—take me out! I'm freezing!" So they took *him* out.

Then they said, "Hamal *Paşa* Hasan, they haven't been able to do it. Only you can do it. Let's tie the rope around your waist and let you down into the well."

Hasan said, "But don't you see? One went down and said he was burning, and the other said he was freezing. What if I get burned or frozen, and die? What will my wife do without me? If I die, will you pay some compensation to my wife?"

And they said, "Yes, yes, we'll compensate your wife for your loss; she'll be paid for it. Instead of having all our cattle die here, we'll do that."

So the chief merchant gave Hasan a bag full of gold, and Hasan put the gold in a big belt and gave it back to him, saying, "In case I am killed, you'll send it to my wife." So they tied the rope around his waist and they let him down into the well. Soon he began to shout, "I'm freezing! I'm freezing!" but they let him go still farther, and he *screamed*, "I'm freezing!" until he came down to the very bottom, where there was the Water of Life.

Then he said, "Send down the buckets!" And they sent the buckets down, and he filled them and they pulled, he filled them and they pulled, and the water came up. They drank—oh, they drank!—and then they had the animals drink all the water they wanted, and they poured water all around the tents, and finally they said, "We have enough. Come up!"

Hasan said, "Let me have a drink for myself before I come up." But before he drank, he looked carefully to see what was around, and he saw a door on his right. He opened the door and went in. There he found a very beautiful girl sitting and embroidering, and there was a frog sitting on the hoop.

"Greetings to you!" said the girl.

And "Greetings to *you!*" said Hasan.

Then the girl said, "Where do you come from? And where are you going?"

He told her where he had come from, and where he was going. And the girl said, "Well, I'll ask you something. Tell me, which of us is the prettier, this frog or I?"

The answer came, "Whomever one loves is the more beautiful."

Then the girl said, "If you hadn't answered my question that way, this was what was going to happen to you. Open the door and see."

Hasan opened another door and he saw a heap of heads. Everyone who had answered differently had had his head cut off by the girl and piled there.

Once more she spoke. "I'm going to give you three pomegranates, and in return you will pretend not ever to have seen me. Just forget about me. When you go home and are with your wife, cut these pomegranates. But, remember, you have never seen me!"

He came out of the room and said, "Let down the rope. I'm coming up." They let down the rope and he tied it around his waist and they pulled him up.

Now he had three pomegranates and a whole beltful of gold, besides. He put these things into a bag and gave them to a very trustworthy man and sent the things home. Then he went on his way.

One day the innkeeper came to the girl's locked room and said, "Here's a package for you, from Hasan." He left the package with her.

When she opened it and saw the gold and the pomegranates, "Oh," she said, "how nice, for the gold. But why did he send me these pomegranates all that way?" As she looked at them, she decided that perhaps a pomegranate would taste good, so she cut one open. As she opened it, she found that it was filled to the brim with jewels, all sorts of jewels. She opened the second pomegranate, and it was filled, just *filled*, with gold.

143

And out of the third pomegranate came a rooster. It said, "*Gahk!*" and jumped on the shelf. And each time it crowed there came gold from it.

In the morning she called the innkeeper and said, "You are my brother, in this world and in the afterworld. This is what I want you to do with me. We'll go out into the market to sell all these jewels and turn them into money."

"All right," said the innkeeper. So they started out. They sold all the jewels that came out of the first pomegranate, and it gave them so much money that they had to carry it back to the inn in huge flour bags. And she still had the gold and the rooster.

Then she said, "Now this is what we are going to do. We are going to have a house as beautiful as a padişah's palace, with all its furniture and with all its decorations, and with all its servants and carriages and dogs, just like my father's palace."

And the innkeeper helped her. He found a house for her as nice as a padişah's palace. He furnished it and found for her the servants and slaves and dogs belonging to a palace. And she settled herself there.

Meanwhile the caravan was on the way back from Baghdad. When they were nearing the city, the girl found out about it, and she called one of her servants. "Get a full set of beautiful clothing, complete with its headdress and fur. Then go to the entrance to the city. You'll find a caravan there. Ask for Hamal Paşa Hasan. Anybody will show him to you. Take him to one side and make him take all his old clothing off and dress him in these clothes and bring him back."

So the servant went to meet the caravan, and, sure enough, the caravan was coming *tungur tingur* with its bells ringing. In front of the caravan was Hamal Paşa Hasan, with his long beard down to his waist, and his boots up to his knees, and his sleeves rolled up. He looked a picture of might.

The servant said, "Greetings be!"

And they answered, "Greetings to you, too!"

Then he said, "I'm looking for Hamal Paşa Hasan. Do you know him?"

And Hasan said, "I am the one."

The servant said, "Brother, step aside, please, and take your clothing off and put these things on."

"What's this? What's happening?" asked Hasan.

"I don't know," said the servant. "Our lady ordered me to do this."

So Hasan took off his clothing and put on the new robes. He rode in the carriage and they started for home, but all the time he was thinking, "How can my wife have all this wealth? Oh, it must be our padişah father helping us!"

When they arrived home the door opened and all the servants met him. The lady had told them to meet their master with due respect, and so they did. They helped him, holding his arms and leading him up the stairs. And all the time he was bewildered. He didn't know what had become of him. Finally they went up to a large room and he was made to sit on down-filled cushions and his wife sat by him. He kept looking at his wife, trying to find out what this was all about, but his wife stopped him from talking, saying, "Later! Later I'll tell you, after the servants have gone from the room."

She ordered the barbers to come and give him a shave, and then she ordered the bath to be made ready, and he went in and bathed. When the food came in, on huge trays, they ate all they wanted.

When everything was finished, they went to bed, and everybody else disappeared. Then they had time to talk to each other all by themselves. "I must know!" said Hasan. "Tell me! Where did we get all these riches?"

And she said, "Well, don't you know? You sent me three pomegranates. I cut one and it was packed full of jewels. And I cut the second one and it was packed full of gold. And I cut the third one and there came out a rooster. Each time the rooster crows, he drops gold. He's in the cupboard. Come and see!"

Then he understood what it was all about, and he felt very, very happy. "You know, wife," he said, "let's do this. Let's call a crier and have him go all through the town and for three days let's invite everyone to come to dinner with us. And we shall give a piece of gold to each guest for the rent of his teeth."

So they had the criers go out, and they ordered the cooks to prepare a banquet—meat and rice and macaroni and vegetables and fruits and everything just *poured* into the house. When the food was cooked, everybody was served. Before they left the house, Hamal Paşa Hasan of the caravan, the host, sat by the door and gave a piece of gold to each guest who had honored their house by coming and eating. He sat by the door in his fur, with his long pipe.

Now when the padişah heard about this house where food was served and people were given money, he called one of his servants and said, "Who *is* this person? Is it possible that he may be richer than I am? Let's go and eat there, like anybody else. I'll go in disguise, so they won't know me. We'll just go and eat there."

So the padişah changed his clothing and they started, like any ordinary people. As they were coming to Hasan's house, the daughter saw him and of course she recognized her own father. She told Hasan, "Look, my father is coming with a servant. He's going to eat here. Be sure to give him *two* pieces of gold instead of one, and one for the servant—*two* for my father, and *one* for the servant."

The padişah was honored just like everyone else. He and his servant were offered food, and when they had had coffee and were ready to leave, Hasan, the host, gave *two* pieces of gold to the padişah and *one* to his servant. After they had left the house, the padişah said, "Why do you suppose they gave me *two* and gave you *one* piece of gold?"

Since the feast was to go on for three days, they decided to go back again the next day, and they did. This time the daughter said to Hasan, "Please tell my father not to leave after eating, but to stay behind."

When the padişah and his servant were ready to leave, Hasan came to the padişah and said, "Please, sir, won't you stay behind for a minute?"

He stayed, and when everyone else was gone, Hasan's wife, the padişah's daughter, came into the room dressed in a most gorgeous gown, with gold all around her neck and with a crown on her head, and her robe was red. As she walked in, Hasan said, "Your Majesty, here is your daughter."

And the padişah said, "No, she is not my daughter."

"But she *is* your daughter," said Hasan.

"No," said the padişah. "My daughter is gone, married to a poor man. This is not my daughter."

"How would you know your daughter? Do you have any sign to know her by?"

"Yes," said the padişah. "Down on her neck there is a mole."

When he said that, she bent before her father and lifted up her hair, and, right enough, there was a mole there, in the same place.

"Well," said the padişah, "I was mistaken. There *is* someone richer than I am. Allah is richer than I am. Listen to me. I am an old man now, and all I have is yours, Hasan. From now on, my crown and my kingdom will be yours. You'll rule in my place. And from today on, I'll spend my time washing and praying."

To celebrate the occasion, they arranged a wedding for forty days and forty nights, all anew, fit for a king, and their wish was fulfilled. Let's go up and sit in their seats.

Riddles

A *mouth* it has, there is no doubt,
But yet a *head* it is without.
What is this thing I ask about?
                    (Bottle)

As you twist its ear, its mouth waters.
                    (Faucet)

I stepped in it and it filled gladly;
I pulled it and it wilted sadly.
                    (Stocking)

Glossary

ALLAH   The Muslim term for *God*.

ALMS   Something given (usually money) to help poor people; almsgiving is one of the five basic requirements of a Muslim.

AMAN!   The Turkish expression said at times of surprise, dismay, or distress; English equivalents could be "Oh!" "Ah!" "Mercy!" "Help!" or "For goodness' sake!"

ASP   A small, very deadly Egyptian snake, similar to a very small cobra.

BAGGY TROUSERS (*şalvar* in Turkish)   Long the traditional dress in rural Turkey, such trousers are warm in winter and cool in summer. Low in the crotch, gathered around the waist, and narrow at the ankles, şalvar provide modest dress for both men and women. Men's şalvar are dark in color and somewhat less baggy; women's şalvar are very colorful, in printed cotton.

BAKLAVA   A highly caloric Turkish and Greek dessert combining many layers of buttered tissue-thin pastry, finely chopped walnuts, and selected spices, and drenched, after baking, with a honeyed syrup.

BIRD OF FORTUNE   A bird belonging to the padişah and released, following the padişah's death, to perch upon the head of the person most suitable to become the next padişah.

BİSMİLLAH! ("I begin with the name of Allah!") This is said to invoke the blessing of Allah on whatever work or venture is being undertaken.

BOHÇA A square piece of cloth used to wrap towels, soap, and clean clothing by women going to a Turkish bathhouse. The four corners are brought together to close the packet but are not tied; the bohça is supported underneath by the hands.

BÖREK Flaky pastry with thin layers of cheese or other filling.

CHUSH! The Turkish word (like the English "Whoa!") intended to direct a horse or a donkey to stop.

COCKCROW AS SIGNAL As soon as the first cock (rooster) crows in the morning, jinns, witches, and ghosts must return to the otherworld.

COVERED BAZAAR A famous covered area in İstanbul housing more than 4,000 shops under one roof.

CRIER A messenger sent out to announce loudly to the public an order or an important piece of news.

DEH! The Turkish word (like the English "Giddap!") intended to direct a horse or a donkey to start moving ahead.

DELİ A Turkish term meaning both "crazy" and "brave to the point of foolishness"; the term is used also as a name.

EFFENDI A term of respect added to a personal name; the closest equivalent in English is "sir."

EYVAH! The Turkish form for "alas!"—an expression of dismay or distress.

FISHER (MARTEN) A larger relative of the weasels, this carnivorous mammal tends to live in trees and to relish fish.

FOUNTAIN In Turkey, this term describes any public source of water, most often provided through a faucet or faucets, rather than the decorative kind that sprays.

GIANTS AND WATER It is widely believed that neither giants nor witches can cross rivers or other flowing water.

HAMAL The Turkish term for "porter," one who carries burdens or bundles for a small fee; large items are carried on a "saddle" resting on the hamal's back and shoulders and secured by a rope.

HAMAM A Turkish public bathhouse to which people go, often for an entire day, not only to bathe but to enjoy themselves with fine foods, conversation, and storytelling. Some hamams have separate days scheduled for men and for women; others have separate sections for men and for women. There is no mixing of sexes at a hamam.

HELVA A dessert or candy made from sesame oil, farina or flour, and syrup or honey; nuts and cinnamon can also be added.

HİÇ! The standard Turkish word for "nothing" or "a mere trifle"; in local dialects, it sometimes has other meanings, such as "salt."

HOCA The Turkish term for a Muslim teacher or preacher; the hoca can teach either in a mosque or in a classroom.

İMAM A prayer leader in a mosque; also, a religious leader in the Muslim faith, called İslam.

JINN (spelled *cin* in Turkish) A djinn, genie, demon, or evil spirit with special power either to help or to hurt; in Turkish tales, the jinn is often described as very large and fearsome.

KEBAB A Turkish meat-and-vegetables dish grilled either on a *şiş* (skewer) with vegetables alternated with the meat (*şiş kebab*) or on a vertical spit that turns slowly before a gas or electric grill, roasting as it turns (*döner kebab*), with salad vegetables served as a relish.

KELOĞLAN A boy or man, bald from a scalp disease, who serves as a popular hero of Turkish folktales; he starts as poor and unknown, but through luck and talent achieves success.

KIOSK (spelled *Köşk* in Turkish) A lightly constructed, elegant, airy house usually occupied as a vacation home by wealthy people.

KÖSE A man with little or no beard and usually with a heart-shaped face, bowed legs, and a high voice; in Turkish tales, he is a villain, extremely untrustworthy.

KURUŞ A small copper coin; 100 kuruş equal one lira.

LİRA The basic Turkish monetary unit; once prized as income, a single lira now is worth less than one-tenth of an American penny. At the time of these folktales, it was still highly valued.

LUK! A Turkish expression suggesting the sound of swallowing when drinking water, or the sound of an object or a fish dropped into water.

MINARET A tall, slender tower attached to a mosque and encircled with one or more balconies from which the five-times-daily call to Muslim prayer is given.

MUEZZIN A Muslim crier who summons the faithful to prayers five times daily from the balcony of a minaret; the summons always includes the same chant.

MUHTAR The only elected official of a village or of a quarter of a town; the head man.

NOONDAY PRAYER The holiest of the five daily Muslim prayer services, with the most important noonday service held on Friday, the traditional Muslim Sabbath.

PADİŞAH Ruler or king of a country or of a class of creatures (padişah of birds, padişah of fairies). Since the padişah had the power of life and death over his subjects, he was usually feared.

PAŞA The highest title of military rank (like "general"), it can be added to a name as a term of respect or flattery.

SADDLEBAG A carpet-fabric saddle cover with a big pocket at each side, it is placed across the back of a horse or a donkey to hold produce or bundles (or gold!).

SASH, OR CUMMERBUND A long, sturdy strip of cloth wrapped several times around the waist of a man or a woman in rural Turkey both to provide support in heavy work and to carry valuables such as money.

SHROUD A long white piece of cloth wound around the corpse of a Muslim after the body has been washed for burial; the body is buried without a coffin.

SİMİT A crisp, breadlike roll shaped in a ring five or six inches across, and sold along the street to be eaten as a snack.

THREE OR FIVE The Turkish expression used to indicate *a few* of anything: days, people, coins, meters.

TOPKAPI PALACE The home of the sultan, and the headquarters for the Ottoman Empire for more than four hundred years, this huge complex is now a museum.

VIZIER An advisor and assistant to a padişah or a sultan.

YOĞURT Original Turkish form of yogurt, the fermented, slightly acid milk-based food found at dairy counters.

YUFKA Bread baked in thin, firm sheets shaped like immense pancakes; it is made in large quantities and stored in piles. Before it is eaten, it is moistened to restore freshness.

ZURNA A simple double-reed instrument usually played along with a drum in folk music, especially for weddings and other festivals.

A Note on the Texts

A number of the folktales and several of the riddles in the present volume appeared initially in print as follows. In all cases, copyright is held by Barbara K. Walker.

"The Mouse and the Elephant" (under "Beth Kilreon"): *Humpty Dumpty's Magazine*, May 1969.

"Hasan, the Heroic Mouse-Child" (as "Hasan-Bey the Mouse-Child"): *Instructor*, October 1969.

"The Magpie and the Milk": *Humpty Dumpty's Magazine*, January 1975.

"The Mosquito and the Water Buffalo," in *Laughing Together: Giggles and Grins from Around the Globe*: UNICEF/Four Winds Press, 1976.

"The Rabbit and the Wolf" (as a playlet): *Humpty Dumpty's Magazine*, November 1962.

"The Lion's Den" (as a playlet): *Humpty Dumpty's Magazine*, July 1962.

"I Know What *I'll* Do"; "Nasreddin Hoca and the Third Shot"; "The Hoca as Tamerlane's Tax Collector"; and "The Hoca and the Candle," in *Watermelons, Walnuts and the Wisdom of Allah and Other Tales of the Hoca*: Parents' Magazine Press, 1967.

"Teeny-Tiny and the Witch-Woman": *Humpty Dumpty's Magazine*, December 1970.

"The Wonderful Pumpkin": *Humpty Dumpty's Magazine,* September 1968.

"The Courage of Kazan" as text for picture book: Crowell, 1971.

"Just Say *Hiç!*" as text for picture book: Follett, 1965.

"Three Tricksters and the Pot of Butter": *Cricket,* April 1977.

"Stargazer to the Sultan" as text for picture book: Parents' Magazine Press, 1967.

"The Bird of Fortune": *Children's Digest,* January 1969.

"The Princess and the Pig": *Humpty Dumpty's Magazine,* September 1973.

"Hamal Hasan and the Baby Day": *Scholastic NewsTime,* March 15, 1971.

"The Round Sultan and the Straight Answer" as text for picture book: Parents' Magazine Press, 1970.

"A Mirror, a Carpet, and a Lemon" (under "Beth Kilreon"): *Humpty Dumpty's Magazine,* February 1970.

"New Patches for Old": *Humpty Dumpty's Magazine,* October 1973.

"Hasan and Allah's Greatness" (as "Keloğlan and God's Greatness"), in *Once There Was and Twice There Wasn't*: Follett, 1968.

Selected riddles, from "Riddles Told in Turkey": *Cricket,* April 1978.